THE COMPLETE GUIDE TO INVESTING FOR TEENS

How to Invest to Start Grow Your Money, Reach Your Financial Freedom and Build Your Smart Future

Warren Miller

Warren Miller

To my Family and
My Little Cookie

© Copyright 2021 - All rights reserved.

The content contained within this book may not be reproduced, duplicated or transmitted without direct written permission from the author or the publisher.

Under no circumstances will any blame or legal responsibility be held against the publisher, or author, for any damages, reparation, or monetary loss due to the information contained within this book. Either directly or indirectly.

Legal Notice:

This book is copyright protected. This book is only for personal use. You cannot amend, distribute, sell, use, quote or paraphrase any part, or the content within this book, without the consent of the author or publisher.

Disclaimer Notice:

Please note the information contained within this document is for educational and entertainment purposes only. All effort has been executed to present accurate, up to date, and reliable, complete information. No warranties of any kind are declared or implied. Readers acknowledge that the author is not engaging in the rendering of legal, financial, medical or professional advice. The content within this book has been derived from various sources. Please consult a licensed professional before attempting any techniques outlined in this book.

By reading this document, the reader agrees that under no circumstances is the author responsible for any losses, direct or indirect, which are incurred as a result of the use of information contained within this document, including, but not limited to, errors, omissions, or inaccuracies.

TABLE OF CONTENTS

INTRODUCTION 8

CHAPTER 1 10 REASONS TO START 10
    DANGER RETURN COMPROMISE 11
    SORTS OF INVESTMENT CHOICES ACCESSIBLE 12

CHAPTER 2 HOW TO EARN YOUR OWN MONEY AND INCREASE YOUR GOALS-BUDGET 14

CHAPTER 3 GETTING AND MANAGING MONEY 18
    WHERE TO PUT YOUR MONEY 18
    SAVINGS ACCOUNTS 18
    CHECKING ACCOUNTS 19
    CERTIFICATES OF DEPOSIT (CDs) 19
    LAWS, TAXES AND TAX-FRIENDLY INVESTMENTS: TIPS FOR PARENTS 19
    IRAs 22

CHAPTER 4 BUSINESS AND FINANCIAL CONCEPTS 24
    NET WORTH 24
    INFLATION 24
    LIQUIDITY 24
    BULL MARKET 24
    BEAR MARKET 25
    RISK TOLERANCE 25
    ASSET ALLOCATION AND DIVERSIFICATION 25
    INTEREST 25
    COMPOUND INTEREST 26
    HOW MARKET WORKS 28

CHAPTER 5 THE RIGHT TIME AND THE RIGHT WAY TO INVEST 30
    WHAT ARE SMART GOALS? 32
    HOW DOES SETTING SMART FINANCIAL GOALS HELP ME ACHIEVE SUCCESS? ... 33
    HOW DO I SET THE BEST FINANCIAL GOALS? 33

CHAPTER 6 UNDERSTANDING AND INVESTING IN BONDS 34
What Is a Bond? 34
When Is the Government Going to Start Paying Back What It Owes? 35
How Do I Know that the Government Is Really Going to Pay Me Back? 35
How Does This Affect Me? 35
How Do I Buy a Bond? 36
What Are My Options for Investing in Bonds? 36
Government Bonds 37

CHAPTER 7 UNDERSTANDING AND INVESTING IN STOCKS 42
When Not to Buy Stocks 44

CHAPTER 8 INDEX AND MUTUAL FUNDS: WHY NOT? 48

CHAPTER 9 EXCHANGE-TRADED FUNDS (ETFS) 56
What Makes an ETF Different? 56
So, What's in an ETF? 57
Equity ETFs 60
Fixed Income ETFs 61
Commodity ETFs 61

CHAPTER 10 OTHER TYPES OF INVESTMENTS 64
Cryptocurrencies 64
Gold and Silver 65
Private Equity 66
Hedge Funds 67
Ethical Investments 68
Coins, Stamps and Art 69
The Purchase of Comic Books 70

CHAPTER 11 HOW TO MANAGE YOUR INVESTMENT PORTFOLIO 72
What Is an Investment Portfolio? 72
Strategy #1: Stay Invested All the Time 73
Strategy #2: Try to Time the Market 73

CHAPTER 12 PERSONAL ADVISOR AND ONLINE BROKERS 76

How to Open a Broker Account 80

CHAPTER 13 BEST INVESTING AND MICRO-SAVINGS APPS 82

Investing Vs Micro-Savings Apps 82
The Best Micro-Savings Apps 83

CHAPTER 14 MISTAKES TO AVOID 90

Five Huge Mistakes that Beginners Make 90
Mistakes that even Good Investors had Made 96

CHAPTER 15 CHAPTER 15. INSIDER'S SECRET OF THE STOCK MARKET 100

CHAPTER 16 SOME OF THE TOP TRADERS IN THE STOCK MARKET 106

Benjamin Graham 106
Warren Buffet 107
Paul Tudor Jones 108
Tim Cook 109
George Soros 110
Carl Icahn 110
John C. Bogle 111

CONCLUSION 114

Risks of Not Investing 117

APPENDIX 120

Recommended Readings and Podcasts 120
One Last Tip for You 122

Warren Miller

Introduction

The benefits of investing early on are enormous: You can get started much sooner than if you start at age 20, at which point many 401(k) accounts locked up until retirement. You'll be able to choose from different investments that grow at different rates so you can try out what fits with your goals. And you'll be able to give your money a head start on the decades ahead.

There are so many reasons to start investing now, not least of all because the stock market has historically returned an average annual rate of 9%. However, if you wait until you're older, other factors come into play. For example, by starting now, you'll have more time to ride out ups and downs and get over your fears of the unknown. When you're young, it's easier to recover from financial setbacks because your personal economy isn't as developed as that of an older investor's. You also can stash away extra money without having to cut back on spending in other areas. And if you invest while you're still in high school, you could get a head start on your retirement and college funds.

Another advantage of investing early is that if you hold on to the investment for many years and decades, your earnings will compound to volumes unachievable if you invest later in life. It's like compounding interest—money reinvested earns money on top of itself—but for stocks. So if you invest $5,000 at age 20 (assuming a 9% return), it will be worth about $131,000 when you're 65.

According to the U.S. Securities and Exchange Commission, "*You learn a lot in the first 20 years of your life. You learn how to eat and sleep, walk and talk about politics, deal with friends, teachers, bosses and coworkers. But there is one thing you don't do a lot of while you are young: Invest.* "Sadly, that's what most teens do: not invest. According to a UBS/Gallup Investor and Retirement Optimism report published on May 2nd in The Washington Post, only 14% of teenagers (ages 13-19) have invested in stocks or stock mutual funds. In comparison, 18% of adults age 30 and older have done so.

What's worse is that most teenagers don't even open a savings account or put money into other long-term investments. According to the UBS/Gallup report, only 40% of 13-19-year-olds have ever opened a savings account, and only 6% have put money into stocks or stock mutual funds. But when you hit your 20s, it's too late to start investing for retirement (at least through a company like Vanguard).

"There are many reasons young people are not investing in the stock market," said Kirk Chisholm of Chisholm Financial Group LLC in McLean, Virginia. *"Some are afraid of losing money; some don't know how much they need to save to reach a particular goal; and some are confused about the right investment vehicles."*

But by investing now, you can learn the ropes of the market before you need your money for retirement. *"It's never too early to begin planning your financial future,"* said Chisholm. *"The sooner that starts, and the more resources invested, the better off you will be when it comes time to use those resources."*

You also have plenty of time to invest in different ways and try new investment strategies. Continue reading to know more!

CHAPTER 1

10 Reasons to Start

To fabricate riches, you ought to invest your cash. On the off chance that you don't invest, you will pass up freedoms to build your monetary worth. Obviously, you can possibly lose cash in investments, however in the event that you invest carefully, the possibility to acquire is higher. If not invested, the purchasing influence of your cash will devalue extra time. Top reasons why you ought to invest your cash are:

1. **Abundance Creation** — Investing your cash will permit it to develop. Most investment vehicles, for example, stocks, testaments of store, or securities, offer profits for your cash over long haul. This return permits your cash to compound, bringing in cash on target previously procured and making abundance over the long haul.

2. **Beat Inflation** — 100 rupees today would just be 96.5 rupees one year from now as per late Indian expansion measurements, which infers that you would lose 4.5% of our cash each year whenever kept as money. Gets back from the investment keeps up the buying power at a consistent level. In the event that you don't beat the swelling rate you'd lose cash, not bringing in cash.

3. **Retirement corpus creation** — An individual ought to invest while he is procuring in order to make a corpus of assets that can be utilized when one resigns. This retirement store gathers extra time and gives security to keep an agreeable way of life even after retirement.

4. **Achieve monetary objectives** — Investing can help you arrive at greater monetary objectives. This profit for your investments can be utilized toward major monetary objectives, for example, purchasing a home, purchasing a vehicle, going into business, or setting up your kids for school.

5. **Duty saving** — Some investment vehicles give a twofold return by giving returns just as lessening your available pay, which thusly limits the expense obligation, for example, value connected reserve funds plot (ELSS) reserves. Cash set aside is cash acquired which can be invested further.

6. **Significant yields** — Investing would assist with accomplishing exceptional yields when contrasted with bank's saving record, which gives a simple 4% return. Investing in business sectors could give you returns as much as 20% whenever given the opportune time skyline.

Actuality: If an individual invested Rs 724 in June 1989, then the sum would have compounded to Rs 34,903 today!

Prior to pushing forward, an investor needs to comprehend the idea of danger return compromise.

Danger Return Compromise

Regardless of whether you are making an investment in value in the securities exchange, land, government bonds or some other monetary instrument, there are these two factors your investment is ensured to have: danger and return. Simply, hazard alludes to the likelihood of bringing about misfortunes comparative with your investment. No investment exists that is totally hazard-free. Return gauges the genuine addition or misfortune your investment creates. While the word return is most regularly connected with an addition, it is completely conceivable to have a negative return, clearly showing a genuine misfortune on your investment. The danger/return tradeoff is consequently an investment rule that demonstrates a connected connection between these two investment factors. The tradeoff is very basic: investments with higher danger are related to a more prominent likelihood of better yield, while investments with lower hazard have a more noteworthy likelihood of more modest return.

Youthful investors ought to have high extent of value in their portfolio as their danger-taking limit is more. More established individuals who are near their retirement age ought not to invest in value yet should search for fixed pay instruments, for example, bonds, debentures and government protections as they would give a constant flow of incomes with least conceivable danger.

Sorts of Investment Choices Accessible

1. **Value** — Stock investments address value proprietorship in a traded on an open market organization. Organizations issue stock as a component of a capital-raising system that subsidizes the activities of the organization. Corporate shares have shifting development prospects and are commonly dissected dependent on attributes, for example, assessed future profit and cost-to-income proportions. Stocks can be ordered in different classifications. Stocks may likewise offer profits adding a pay payout segment to the investment.

2. **Fixed Income Instruments** —Bonds are perhaps the most notable fixed pay items. They can be offered by governments or organizations. They are likewise given as a feature of an organization's capital-raising system. Bonds pay investors premium as coupon installments and offer full head reimbursement at development. Securities are ordinarily evaluated by a FICO assessment office, which offers understanding of their capital construction and capacity to make opportune installments.

3. **Favored Shares** — are ideal option for hazard opposed value investors in light of the fact that these are portions of an organization's stock with profits that are paid out to investors, before regular stock profits are given.

4. **Common Funds** — are comprised of a pool of assets gathered from numerous investors to invest in protections, for example, stocks, securities, currency market instruments and comparable resources. Shared assets are worked by cash directors who invest the asset's capital and endeavor to deliver capital additions and pay for the asset's investors.

5. **Subsidiaries** — Derivatives are investment items that are offered dependent on the development of a predetermined fundamental resource. Put or call choices on stocks and fates dependent on the development of items costs are the most widely recognized type of subordinate investment.

CHAPTER 2

How to Earn Your Own Money and Increase Your Goals-Budget

So, you're sixteen or older and you still live with your parents. Maybe you do a bit of work around the house like cleaning or doing the dishes, but don't feel like you can make your voice heard when it comes to what food should be on the dinner table tonight.

Or maybe your parents are just not interested in meeting your needs. The good news is that there are many ways for teenagers to have some fun and earn their own money. Here's how:

- **Pocket Money.** Ask for a small weekly allowance at home by giving an example of the things they would pay for with their money (like books, movies, clothes). If parents are not in a position to give you any money, ask for something else (like spending money, lunch at the school, etc.).

- **Summer Jobs.** Work on your own after school. You can do volunteer work or babysit. Check out companies near your house that hire teenagers.

- **Get a "Real Job".** Try to be a supervisor for your favorite fast food place or supermarket, or get a job at a local mall.

- **Add Work Experience.** Ask around for part-time jobs you can do during the summer holidays or on vacations: busboy, salesman, pizza delivery boy, etc.

- **Work in the "Growth" Economy.** Advertise for a part-time job at your local business and ask if they can give you a ride there. If you're under eighteen, have your teacher or others call the business for you. Many businesses will hire teens, sign them up for work experience with no pay and then ask them to come back part-time when school reopens.

- **Start a Business.** You can start a business with your friends. You can invite your friends to help and be the boss. If you're under eighteen, check with the school or parents first because businesses will not hire teens unless they are old enough to be able to work legally and have a Social Security number.

- **Gifts from relatives.** You may find that some relatives will give you money for your birthday or Christmas. It could be a nice surprise to open up present and find some cash in the card envelope!

- **Summer Jobs.** Many people do part-time jobs during the summer. This is one of the most common ways for teens to make money. Many students work in gas stations or restaurants and can earn enough money to buy gifts for themselves and their friends.

- **Selling things that you no longer need**. You probably have many items around your house which are used but still have some value. If your parents aren't using an item, why not sell it at a yard sale? You could get some extra money from these items and donate some of it to charity (or spend it yourself!).

- **Babysitting.** Many parents ask their friends and relatives for recommendations of babysitters. Invite them over for dinner or ask them to meet you at an event and they will become more likely to give you their contact information or ask for yours.

You can add this information to your own contacts and start babysitting when they're out of town. It's a simple way of making money, but can be very rewarding!

- **If you have an online presence, you could make money from advertising revenue.** Online advertisers often pay for advertising based on the amount of views or clicks your website receives from users who access it through links they place on their site.

Warren Miller

CHAPTER 3

Getting and Managing Money

Where to Put Your Money

Most teens have part-time jobs, babysitting jobs, or allowance they earn from helping out around the house. That money needs to be put to work for teens' long-term future. They can't afford to just put the money in a piggy bank or under their mattress and forget about it. Here are some options parents should discuss with their teens before deciding what to do with their savings.

Savings Accounts

Savings accounts are the most commonplace for teens to save their money. Many banks offer different types of savings accounts:

- Interest-bearing accounts may pay teens a little bit of interest (meaning they earn a small percentage of the amount in the account).

- No-fee accounts may earn the same interest as interest-bearing accounts, but they don't come with any fees.

- Online savings accounts can be more convenient than traditional bank branches, as you can transfer money quickly and pay bills online.

It's important to compare different options and make sure you understand what the fees are for each option so you can decide what's best for your family.

Checking Accounts

Another option is a checking account that offers savings features. It allows teens to have a checking account like adults but also earn interest on their money.

While most checking accounts don't usually earn a lot of interest, there is a new type of checking account that does. It's called a high-yield checking account. With this type of account, teens can earn more interest than with traditional savings accounts and have the convenience of a checking account, including being able to make withdrawals and deposits at anytime and anywhere, using ATMs or bank branches.

Certificates of Deposit (CDs)

A certificate of deposit is similar to a savings account in that it generally offers higher interest rates than other investment options (though CDs are not usually as liquid). CDs require a certain amount of money to be deposited for periods ranging from one month up to five years. If the money is withdrawn before the end of the deposit period, it may result in a penalty.

Laws, Taxes and Tax-Friendly Investments: Tips for Parents

What are custodial accounts?

Custodial accounts are created for minors (children under 18). These accounts can be either set up by parents or grandparents and allow the child access to his money. If a minor has earned income, such as delivering newspapers, babysitting or working part-time at McDonald's, that money can be deposited into his custodial account and used for whatever the child sees fit. Or it can be used to pay for an education.

Why would you want to set up a custodial account?

Perhaps the best reason is that you want to give your child a head start in learning about managing money. It is an excellent opportunity to both learn and practice a variety of financial skills, from saving to making investment decisions. Your child will learn that money is a finite, valuable resource that must be used wisely. The custodial account provides a neat tax shelter as well. You can deposit up to $1,900 annually into the account on behalf of your child. That amount grows tax-deferred until it is withdrawn by your child when he reaches the age of majority (18 or 21 depending on state laws). To open a custodial savings account, the parent must open an individual account in his own name and fund it with $50 worth of U.S. series EE savings bonds. Or you can make a cash deposit into the account. You will then need to obtain a custodial savings certificate with the name of the child and file it with your state's office of securities.

You can take advantage of all the same tax-advantaged accounts for your children as you do for yourself: IRAs, 401(k)s, SEPs, Keoghs and Profit-Sharing Plans. You can direct up to $1,900 annually to these accounts on behalf of your child. The money is taxed when it is taken out by the child at age 18 or 21 depending on state laws. In some cases, it might be advantageous to set up these accounts in the child's name rather than the parent's. This would allow you to avoid "kiddie tax" on investment income over $1,900. If you expect your child to have investment income greater than that amount, it might be wise to explore this option with an accountant or financial planner.

What are UGMA and UTMA accounts?

These are Uniform Gifts to Minors Act and Uniform Transfers to Minors Act accounts, which allow parents or grandparents to make gifts of money or stock directly to a minor. Any income or growth is taxed in the hands of the minor as if he had earned it. UGMA and UTMA accounts are useful where the parents or grandparents don't have much in the way of a taxable income. (You can make only one outright gift per year to an individual regardless of how many accounts he holds.) This is also an easy way for grandparents to provide assistance for grandchildren's higher education expenses without having to worry about annual gift tax limits. Opening an UGMA or UTMA account is a very simple process. The deed or title of the assets must be transferred into the name of someone over 18 years old with "custodian" written in parenthesis next to his name. For example: Joe Blow, custodian for John Doe. The custodian can be either the parent or another adult that the child trusts (such as an aunt or uncle). A parent or caregiver must open an individual account in his name and deposit $50 worth of U.S. savings bonds into it. Then the assets —stocks, a bank account, etc. — are transferred to the individual account named in the deed of trust by your bank or broker.

UGMA and UTMA accounts are a great way to start teaching kids about money from a young age. They are particularly appropriate for children who have special needs or disabilities because they allow parents to help them with their financial affairs without going through a court procedure for guardianship. If the child turns 18 and uses all of the money, he can simply transfer any unused assets back into his own name or a new account. When you set up UGMA or UTMA accounts for your children, it is important to include a brief letter with them explaining why you set up these accounts. A lawyer could draft such a letter for you if you wish. The purpose of including this letter with your offspring's securities is to alert the child, if she ever questions her holdings that someone loves and cares about her. It will also explain what is expected of her if and when it comes time to use these assets. One possible scenario is that the child may need some money for an emergency and she is completely unprepared. If she doesn't understand the purpose of an UGMA or UTMA account, it could create a situation where she may misuse your assets. The letter can also provide a list of talking points to have with her if she chooses to discuss this issue with her friends or instructors.

For example, you might write:

"I've set aside some money for you as a way to help you through school. You can use it to finish your education or to start out in a career. I've written out a list of options for you. You will need to do some serious thinking and planning before you use any of it:

- *Pay tuition for the rest of your undergraduate education*
- *Pay for graduate school*
- *Start a business*
- *Buy a car or home*

If you choose to take some money out, please remember that this is on top of your regular income and expenses. Please see me and we can discuss how this might affect your other funds. Also keep in mind that the principal is what matters most and I hope you will think long term about how best to use it.

If you take some money out, please let me know how it helps so I can put it in your file".

IRAs

Joy is a hard worker. Although she didn't finish high school, she found a stable job. She worked as a warehouse manager for thirty long years. The pay is good, but she ended up spending all she got. When she finally retired, she only saved up $10,000, which only covers a few months of her living expenses. Her pension benefits are simply not enough.

Unfortunately, Joy's story is not unique. More and more retirees are broke.

To avoid ending up like Joy, it is best to invest in an IRA.

IRA or Individual Retirement Account is a tax-advantaged investment and a savings account that allows you to save for retirement.

There are different types of IRA, namely—traditional IRA, Roth IRA, Simple IRA, Spousal IRA, nondeductible IRA, SEP IRA, and self-directed IRA. You will be able to evaluate which seems to be more convenient according to your and your children's needs.

CHAPTER 4

Business and Financial Concepts

Net Worth

Net worth is the value of all of a person's assets subtracting the value of their liabilities. Assets are things such as cash, stocks, bonds, mutual funds, products held for sale in the business (inventory), real estate and other property. Liabilities are accounts payable such as mortgage payments and other debts.

Inflation

Inflation is a sustained increase in the general level of prices for goods and services, where the rate of price increase is higher than in previous periods. It is also a decrease in the purchasing power of money, which means that you need more money to buy a given product or service.

Liquidity

Liquidity is the degree to which an asset or security can be quickly bought or sold in the market without affecting the asset's price.

Bull Market

A buyer market alludes to a market that is on the ascent, which is something to be thankful for. That implies that costs of offers in the market are expanding.

Generally, a positively trending market likewise implies the economy is in a decent state, and the degree of joblessness is low. The US is at present in a positively trending market.

Bear Market

A bear market is something contrary to bull. As such, the market is declining. Offer costs are diminishing, the economy is in a destruction, and joblessness levels are rising.

Risk Tolerance

Risk tolerance is a term used in investment, finance, and economics to describe the amount of uncertainty that an individual or an institution will be able to endure. A high-risk tolerance indicates that the individual or entity can handle volatile markets and maintain their investments during downturns.

Asset Allocation and Diversification

Asset allocation and diversification are two investment strategies that are used to minimize the risk of an investment portfolio. These strategies can be implemented in a number of ways but the common goal is to reduce overall portfolio volatility.

Interest

Interest is a cost incurred as the result of borrowing money from another individual or company. If you borrow $5,000, you may pay back $7,000 after four years. The difference between the two numbers (the original loan and what is owed) is your total interest that is more than doubled. A person might get an interest-free loan if they are living in poverty or have low credit and would otherwise find it difficult to secure a loan on their own.

Compound Interest

Compound interest is when interest earned on a deposit or loan accrues and compounds, so that the compounding occurs not only on the initial amount but also on past earnings (so that it "grows from itself"). This means that compound interest can cause the total to increase exponentially, rather than arithmetically.

Interest, or simple interest, is an aggregate you pay for having utilized a monetary assistance: for example, the interest you pay to the bank for a home loan or any loan specified. As you most likely are aware, the longer the span of the loan, the more prominent the general interest you pay to the bank, in light of the fact that the last will take more time to gather the whole sum that has been progressed to you.

We should make a qualification quickly: simple or compound interest?

Simple interest is the one characterized above, while compound interest will be interest on interest.

We contextualize simple interest and compound interest both in the realm of monetary investments, which is the thing that interests us explicitly. Simple interest is the return that is paid to you reliably, in light of an underlying invested capital, which doesn't increment since you intermittently pull out the profit.

I'll give you a solid model. Invest an amount of $20,000 in an instrument with which you procure 10% per annum, you will get yourself an amount of $22,000 toward the year's end; in this way pull out the $2,000 of benefit and rehash a similar investment with the underlying capital consistently of $20,000.

Following 10 years, you will get yourself $40,000, or you will have multiplied the underlying capital.

Compound interest, then again, depends on the ceaseless reinvestment of the collected profit, without the withdrawal toward the year's end.

Take a similar model again yet, in the wake of procuring $2,000 in the principal year, invest the total amassed capital in the subsequent year, for example the amount of $22,000 and not $20,000 as in the primary model.

The underlying invested capital will step by step increment after every year and subsequently the yearly profit will increment appropriately.

In this subsequent case, following 10 years you will procure $51,875.

In the picture underneath you can perceive what occurs in the two instances of simple interest and compound interest.

	Initial Investment	$20.000
	Annual interest rate	10,00%
	Investment duration (years)	10

Future value with simple interest: 20.000+(20.000*10%)*10 =		$40.000
Future value with compound interest without P.A.C.: VF=20.000*(1+10/1)^10 =		$51.875
	Simple net interest	$20.000
	Net compound interest without P.A.C.	$31.875

	Int. Simple	Int. Compound without PAC
Total capital	$40.000	$51.875
Interest only	$20.000	$31.875

Do you comprehend the significance of compound interest and for what reason do you need to utilize it to acquire it over the long run? Disregard simple interest and from this point forward stress over taking advantage of compound interest in your investments.

The power of compounding interest is one of the most useful financial tools at one's disposal. First and foremost, it stresses the importance of saving money from early on to maximize the total amount obtained later in life. Secondly, it uses compound interest to reach the ambitious goal of amassing $500,000.00 by the time one's life is over. Thirdly, it emphasizes that not only does one need a lot of money saved up but also must follow the advised system of putting aside money without interruption. If one quits saving after just five years then they will have accumulated less than $100,000.00! The power of compounding interest is powerful but not every investment plan can survive in its wake. It is important to avoid risky investments and to stick with those that are more stable like bonds and savings accounts that traditionally have higher interest rates than other types of investments.

How Market Works

The first question you probably have is what causes these fluctuations in the first place. The answer is a little more complex than most people think. It is true that there are many factors that can cause market changes, but they're a response to changes in consumer demand, which is actually caused by inflation and unemployment rates. Yes, it's about supply and demand; we all know about this concept, right? Rest assured, these concepts aren't just complicated for complicatedness' sake! Instead, they help you understand how market movements occur and how you can use them to your advantage when trading or investing. When you go out and purchase something, you're creating demand. You put money into the economy, and that money goes into someone else's pocket. That person then uses it to buy a candy bar or a new pair of shoes, and then he or she might spend that money on beer or cigarettes. This endless cycle eventually creates inflation. What does this have to do with markets? Well, when you see market shifts, they're usually triggered by changes in inflation or unemployment rates. Investors will sell their stocks or bonds if they are worried that inflation is going to rise and may make those investments worthless.

Unemployment and inflation rates are caused by various factors, such as technological advances or the global economy, which means that you can't predict them from looking at the news. However, one thing is certain: if these rates change drastically in a short period of time, investors will sell their stocks because of the possibility of more inflation. You might be wondering how a change in unemployment rates would create a change in market behavior, but this is actually very straightforward if you understand how governments usually deal with these problems. When an economy suffers from high levels of unemployment, the government will often engage in expansionary fiscal policy, which means they are borrowing money to stimulate spending. As a result of borrowing money, interest rates will fall because there's more cash chasing after bonds; this can stimulate more spending and economic activity. In response to this, inflation will rise a bit. Once the economy is stimulated, investors feel more comfortable investing their money in those companies that are doing well.

CHAPTER 5

The Right Time and the Right Way to Invest

Investing is not a game, and it's time to start playing by the rules. You need to understand the risks, find the right environment, and manage your allocation. If you've ever talked about investing with someone who has made a lot of money in business or on Wall Street, odds are they have a wealth management team backing them up who takes care of all this complicated stuff for them. But what if you do it? In order for investing to work for you, you need to educate yourself before making any decisions about where your money should go. The investment world will capitalize on your ignorance, and you'll lose money. So, where do you start?

How about with the right time and the right way?

First, there's the right time. What do I mean by this? Investing is not a get-rich-quick scheme. It's a slow, steady process that can take years to really pay off — if it pays off at all. Don't be in a hurry to reach your goals; that will just put undue stress on you. Take your time and do it right.

Next, there's the right way. The right way to invest is to follow the rules—and not your emotions. If you are thinking of buying a stock, ask yourself why you want to buy it. Is it because you have done a lot of homework and know the company or is it just because the stock price has gone up (and who doesn't want that)? The answer is probably the latter. The best investors spend 80% of their time doing research and 20% doing everything else—such as buying stocks—and they don't buy anything until they are prepared to do so because they are looking at what's happening with the company.

Buying on emotion is how people lose money, and it's exactly what most investors do. Don't let this be you. Investing is a scary word for many because it seems so daunting. With people living longer, the need to put away money for your retirement is more pressing than ever. That's where we come in! Here are five easy steps on how to invest in the right way, so you can sleep well at night knowing that your finances are safe and sound:

1) Educate yourself about investing and take some time to thoroughly consider what you want from your investment account. Knowing what kind of investment product will work best for you will allow for making a better decision when it comes time to invest as there won't be as many unknowns about possible outcomes of investments or potential risks involved with these potential investments.

2) Once you have a better understanding of the different types of investments available, it's time to compare the costs. This includes analyzing what it will cost on an annual basis to maintain the investment and any other possible fees that may be associated with the investment product as a whole.

3) Calculate your goals and figure out how much you need for your savings. Depending on your budget, determine whether or not you can afford to save a certain amount each month to reach this goal. If your budget doesn't allow for monthly contributions, you can still start saving by making one lump sum payment every so often (e.g.: 3 or 4 times a year).

4) Always do your research on potential investments to be sure that they meet your criteria and needs. As with anything else, knowledge is power.

5) Once you have chosen which investment will work best for you, it's time to get started! Remember that the sooner you invest, the greater your returns will be over the long term. If however, you have many immediate concerns (mortgage payments or college tuition), make sure to invest what is most important first and then build up from there.

What Are SMART Goals?

SMART is an acronym that describes a goal-setting formula that has been proven to be highly effective in helping people achieve their goals.

The acronym stands for:

- **S**pecific: Try to be clear and specific with what you want. The narrower your goal, the more you'll understand the steps necessary to reach it.
- **M**easurable: Set measurable milestones along your way will give you the opportunity to evaluate or correct your steps. When you achieve your milestones, always remember to reward yourself even in small ways.
- **A**ttainable: Setting goals you can reasonably achieve within a certain timeframe will help keep you motivated and focused.
- **R**elevant: Each of your goals should align with your values and larger, long-term goals.
- **T**ime-specific: An end-date will help you prioritize and can provide motivation.

By adhering to these standards, you can make sure that whatever financial goals you set for yourself will be achievable. Once you have set your goals, it is important that you take action immediately to keep them from being forgotten.

How Does Setting SMART Financial Goals Help Me Achieve Success?

The key element of SMART goal-setting is specificity. If you set a goal that is too broad, it will be hard to measure whether you have achieved it. For example, if your goal is to save up money for a down payment for a house, that may be very difficult to achieve unless you set the date of when you plan on buying your house. By setting specific financial goals and deadlines, it will be much easier to monitor your progress. You will also find that other elements of SMART goal-setting will help you achieve financial success.

By keeping track of your goals and keeping them relevant to your life and needs, you can make sure they are attainable, and by making them time-specific, you make sure that they are something which must be completed in a timely manner.

How Do I Set the Best Financial Goals?

First, you must decide what your goal is. There are many ways in which people can set financial goals. If you are saving a lot of money, you may want to set a goal for how much you want to save by the end of each month. If you are trying to pay off debt, it may be best to focus on how much debt you can pay off by the end of each month or how much interest and principal payments will be made towards a specific debt at the end of three months. If your goal is ultimately to save up for retirement, 3–5 years would be a good timeframe in which to work towards that goal. By thinking about what your goals are, you can determine whether it is worth the time and effort to set a specific goal or if you should just be saving what you can.

CHAPTER 6

Understanding and Investing in Bonds

If you have an investment portfolio, there's a good chance that some of your holdings are in bonds.

But if you're not sure what bonds are, how they work, or how you can learn more about them, don't worry! We'll answer the most common questions and get you up to speed with this basic introduction to understanding and investing in bonds.

What Is a Bond?

A bond is basically like getting an IOU from the government (or another entity). The entity creates a document stating that it owes someone X dollars on Y date.

When the entity pays back what it owes at maturity date (which could be any time over 20 years), it pays back with interest.

What is the government selling bonds for?

The government's main reason for selling bonds is to raise money for various projects. They sell bonds at a set rate of interest to investors, who receive periodic interest payments and then get paid back with the principal when the bond matures.

When Is the Government Going to Start Paying Back What It Owes?

The government usually sells bonds with a maturity of 10 years or less. Of course, that means that if you buy a 30-year bond, you'll be getting your principal back when you're in your 50s.

How Do I Know that the Government Is Really Going to Pay Me Back?

You can think of bonds as similar to what happens when you buy a house. The bank will lend you the money, but it will use your house as collateral. If you don't pay the money back, the bank can foreclose and take your house. Similarly, if a country doesn't pay its bondholders back, or only pays them back with another bond (called a "debt swap"), there are consequences. Because bonds are traded on exchanges (like stocks), their value changes based on supply and demand and interest rates. If a government makes bondholders wait too long to get their principal back, they can ask the government for a lower interest rate. This means that the government will pay less interest, and that is one way that it can be forced to pay back its debt at a faster rate.

How Does This Affect Me?

If you buy a bond (and there are many different kinds of bonds), you would collect interest on your investment from the entity that owes you money. You'll get paid at regular intervals (every 6 months in the case of US treasury bonds), and when the bond matures, you would get back your principal (again, this could be ten years in the future).

How Do I Buy a Bond?

If you'd like to be an investor in bonds, you need to do two things. First, you need to decide which country or entity you want to be invested in. This is called making a "country allocation". In the US, bonds can be bought at your local bank or at any brokerage. They can also be traded on exchanges like stocks (for example, you could buy IBM bonds and sell Apple bonds). Bonds pay interest every 6 months (or other regularly occurring intervals).

What Are My Options for Investing in Bonds?

There are many different kinds of bonds with different payouts and risks associated with them. Depending on your goals and risk tolerance, you might want to choose different types of bonds. US Treasury Bonds (often called T-Bonds) are considered very low risk. They have a "AAA" rating and are backed by the US government. This means that if the entity that owes you money (the US government) falls behind in payment, the US will step in to pay its bondholders. T-bonds are easy, safe investments but pay low-interest rates.

Corporate bonds (corporate IOUs) have a lower risk than T-bonds because corporations will not be bailed out by the government if they fall behind on their payments. However, their risk is still higher than T-bonds. Their interest rates are higher as well.

Municipal bonds are issued by state and local governments, and they're considered to have the lowest risk of default of any bonds because the entities that issue them can always raise taxes if they need more money. They pay lower interest rates than corporate bonds but higher interest rates than T-bonds. As you can see, there are many different kinds of bonds, with a wide range of risks and potential returns associated with each kind of bond. Luckily, there are financial advisors that can help you sort through the options available to find ones that work for you and your goals.

Government Bonds

Bonds issued by the federal government are called government bonds and are considered to be risk-free investments. Unlike corporate bonds, government bonds don't have any credit risk attached to them because you know that the issuer is guaranteed by the federal government. Bonds issued by corporations, on the other hand, can default and usually do so without any warning! Because of this higher credit risk, corporate bonds offer a higher yield than their safer counterparts.

Corporate Bonds

Corporate bonds are debt securities issued by companies (rather than governments) to borrow money from investors at a future date with an agreement to pay out at least some interest over time and then repay the principal amount borrowed at maturity. The borrower pays the lender an interest rate that is set at the time of issuance based on the creditworthiness of the company. The riskier the company, or lower its credit rating, the higher (or "riskier") a yield you can expect from buying that company's bonds. Corporate bonds are generally much more volatile in value than government bonds due to their higher risk, however they offer higher yields as well.

Corporate Bonds also trade actively on what's known as the "secondary market" while Government Bonds are traded mostly on what's known as the "primary market".

The most common way to purchase bonds is through brokerage accounts. There are a number of large brokerages which cater to individual investors, making it easy to place trades for as little as a few hundred dollars. Some brokerages even have minimums as low as $1 for bond trades. The other way to invest in bonds is through mutual funds that invest in corporate and government bonds. Investors can buy into these funds with just a few hundred dollars. The fees associated with mutual funds, however, take away from any returns on your investment in the fund. These fees can eat away at the gains you make on the investment and may even make it unprofitable in some cases. There are many types of bonds (corporate, government) that may be worth considering for investment. For example, US Savings Bonds are issued by the US Treasury. These bonds pay a fixed interest rate every six months until they mature 30 years from the issue date. Some Savings Bonds may be cashed in before maturity, but at a steep loss as compared to what could have been earned had the full term been held to maturity.

Corporate bonds come in many different types of ratings and price points. High-quality corporate bonds that carry high credit ratings from Standard & Poor's or Moody's are usually considered to be safer than lower-credit rated corporate bonds. The lower the credit rating, also known as the corporate bond's "credit spread," the higher the yield an investor may expect to receive.

The greater the risk, however, is usually accompanied by a greater expected return. High-risk bonds (i.e. junk bonds) can pay double-digit yields but also have a high likelihood of default.

This is the perfect time to learn about bonds—because know-how could save you a boat load of money! Read on to find out when it makes sense, and when it doesn't, to invest in bonds.

Bonds are for more than just old people: they can be used strategically by young people too. They provide a tax benefit and can be a good way to diversify your portfolio. But before you buy any bonds, there are some things you need to know. Bonds are not all the same—there is a difference between "securities" and "obligations," with securities being riskier than obligations. Plus there are short-term bonds and long-term bonds, and how you choose to use these will affect your return. Since bonds do not have the same liquidity as stocks, you need to know when is a good time to buy them —and when it's not. You also need to have an understanding of how bond prices are determined— and this understanding can only come from practice and experience. Most importantly, you must learn the basics of portfolio construction so that you can determine the appropriate mix of stocks and bonds for yourself. This means learning about risk assessment, asset allocation, diversification, and more.

The market value of a bond depends on several factors: the maturity, the coupon rate, and most importantly—the credit rating. Yield to maturity determines the approximate price at which a security will trade in the open market. Also called interest-rate characteristics, yield to maturity tells us how much interest investors will receive before the bonds reach full maturity date. The more risk you are willing to take, the higher the bond yield will be.

The price of a bond is determined by its coupon rate and the yield to maturity. The price of a bond goes up as its yield goes down (or conversely, as its price goes up as its yield goes down). Trading volume and volatility also affect the bond's price. If there is any uncertainty about the payment of interest or principal amount at maturity, then bonds are less likely to be traded for their full value. This uncertainty usually results from a lower rating or from a high degree of financial leverage in the issuing firm (i.e., after-tax profit less total interest expense divided by gross debt equals 5%). The value of a bond increases when its duration is reduced.

A bond's maturity date determines the length of time that you are investing in the debt obligations of an entity. Bonds have a place in every portfolio, given that they offer tax advantages and interest income. When bonds are used as a short-term financial instrument, then they should seek capital gains and return on investment (ROI).

Bonds are also used as part of the asset allocation process among investors; however, this type of strategy can lead to losses if the investor is not knowledgeable about these instruments. Bonds are also used as a longer-term investment and are particularly useful as a way to diversify one's portfolio. This kind of bond is used when an investor is concerned about the liquidity of the stock market. These bonds move in the opposite direction of stocks and provide an investor with an additional form of diversification. When short-term interest rates increase, then long-term interest rates usually increase correspondingly. Bond prices and yields move inversely to one another given that bonds are traded through yield.

Warren Miller

CHAPTER 7

Understanding and Investing in Stocks

Stocks are a type of financial instrument, and when you invest in them, you're buying shares of ownership in a company. You may not have heard of many of the companies we'll talk about here, but they employ thousands of people and make products that you consume every day. In fact, it's possible that the companies on our list are even part of your portfolio already! When you buy a share or stock in a company, there are two things at work: company earnings or profits, and the value (or price) that the market places on these profits. What are earnings? Well, they're simply what the company makes selling its products—think about how much profit any store owner makes by selling shoes. This is company earnings.

Now, the other factor involved in buying a stock is what the market will pay for these profits. What does that mean? When you buy a stock, you are effectively agreeing to pay a certain price for the portion of ownership that you are purchasing. The market dictates how much your stock is worth based on how profitable that company is and how much investors think its profits will increase (or decrease) in the future. Today, we'll focus on earning potential and growth so that we can better understand how you make money with stocks. We'll also discuss the ways to invest in stocks. It's important to understand that you're not always going to buy a full share of stock, but rather a small percentage. In fact, most stocks are broken down into two or more shares for every one sold! You've probably heard of people "diversifying" their portfolios. This means that rather than putting all of your eggs in one basket—or investing in just one type of stock—you're spreading out your money. When you diversify, you are offering yourself options so that if the company whose stock you bought has a rough quarter (or year), your portfolio won't become immediately worthless. To diversify, invest in stocks from a variety of companies in different sectors. If you're looking to invest directly with the company, it's often a good idea to search for its financial information in advance so that you know exactly how much your investment is worth. You'll also need to decide whether or not you want your shares in common, preferred or limited form.

Here are the differences:

- **Common Stock**: This is the most traditional type of stock and it's generally worth more when the company is doing well. Many professional investors prefer to buy this stock because it's liquid (i.e., easy to sell and usually not restricted in any way).

- **Preferred Stock:** This is debt that the company owes you, but with a couple of big exceptions. The company isn't legally obligated to pay your dividends until they have paid off their debt, so your money is at risk until that time comes. Also, when the company goes bankrupt, you will be paid before those with common stock—but after those with bonds or preferred debt.

- **Limited Stock:** This is a hybrid between preferred and common stocks, as it offers some of the benefits of both while keeping some of the risks (and potential rewards) associated with each type. There is much less of this type of stock available than the other two, but it can be a good choice if you like the company and want to invest in its future.

When should you be buying stocks? And when should you be selling them? These are questions most investors ask themselves at some point in their investing careers. You'll often hear people say that timing the market is impossible, but that's not true. There are certain times of the year when stocks perform better than others, and there are many reasons why this is so. In this article I'm going to answer the question "when to buy and sell stocks". If you're a value investor, you look for stocks with a low price/book value ratio and/or a low price/earnings ratio. These are the kind of companies that usually outperform the general market. But simply buying these stocks doesn't guarantee you'll make money. When you buy a stock, your return is directly related to how much money is made by the company. This in turn depends on when is the right time of year to buy stocks. Stock prices fluctuate throughout the year, but it's not random. Stock markets tend to perform better during specific periods of the year, and this has been proven by numerous studies over many years around the world. For example, stocks in the United States tend to perform better from October through April. This is known as the October Effect. The reason for this is that people look to rebalance their portfolios in December after all their summer spending, and they like to buy stocks when there's more money in the market. That means demand is high for stocks which improve their price performance. But here's the real question... Is it worth doing? Some people say that timing the market is worth the effort while others argue it's a waste of time. I say it depends on your investment style. If you're a value investor, then I recommend looking at historical stock trends and trying to time your buying accordingly. After all, if you can get better performance without much risk with very little work, then why not? This way of investing is called passive investing and has been around for a long time. It's the basis of many investment strategies like dollar-cost averaging. It's also very simple and easy to understand, which is why so many people use it even though so few people actually succeed.

When Not to Buy Stocks

If you're not a value investor, then timing your stock purchases is probably a waste of time. If the prices are high, don't buy the stocks because you think they'll go even higher. Buying high and selling low isn't smart investing. It's gambling and the odds are against you. Don't try to time the market by buying at the lowest prices because that seldom works out well either unless you know what you're doing and have an edge in trading like day traders do. When in doubt, the middle ground is always the best choice. That's the way the average investor should play it, because if you're not a value investor and you try to time your stock purchases too much, then you're likely to lose money rather than gain it. Additionally, On the off chance that you invested $1,000 in Amazon or Apple 10 years prior, that investment would have truly paid off. As per individual budget site DQYDJ, an underlying $1,000 investment in those organizations in 2008 would be valued at $16,239 and $8,587, separately, as of January 16. On the off chance that you invested $1,000 in Google in a similar time span, it would have paid off, as well. As indicated by DQYDJ, GOOGL would be valued at $3,660 as of January 16 and GOOG would be valued at $2,008. (Google's stock split into two classes in 2014: GOOGL: Alphabet Class An and GOOG: Alphabet Class C.) All things considered, the information shows that one company altogether beat Amazon, Apple and either class of Alphabet: Netflix. As of January 16, a $1,000 investment in the video-web-based feature would merit an incredible $70,263.

Netflix first dispatched its real-time feature in 2007, started delivering unique substance in 2013 and has developed its endorser base to almost 120 million records around the world. The company likewise added in excess of 8,000,000 supporters in the final quarter, CNBC reports, fundamentally more than Wall Street assumptions, and its shares have bounced in excess of 8%, bringing its market capitalization above $100 billion interestingly. The company intends to burn through $7.5–8 billion on substance in 2018, including shows from titan Shonda Rhimes and comic book company Millarworld. *"We accept our enormous investments* in *substance are paying off,"* the company wrote in a letter to shareholders.

Be that as it may, while Netflix's stock has performed well and the company has high expectations for the future, any individual stock can over—or fail to meet expectations. Past returns don't foresee future outcomes. Furthermore, there are a few difficulties not too far off. Contenders, like Disney, which has consented to purchase 21st Century Fox resources, might actually pull watchers from Netflix with plans to dispatch their own web-based features.

Disney's arrangement with Fox would give the consolidated company a stake in Netflix's adversary, Hulu. Furthermore, Amazon, Apple, Facebook and YouTube have added more substance to their separate stages.

So a few investors are bearish— Jim Cramer, host of CNBC's "Frantic Money," however, isn't one of them. With Netflix raising the month-to-month cost for its web-based feature and adding more unique substance to supplement effectively well-known shows like *"The Crown"* and *"More unusual Things,"* Cramer, in October, said the company could quicken its development significantly further.

Ted Sarandos, Netflix's main substance official, said he would not like to get *"excessively diverted by* the *serious scene".* The company concurs. *"The market for amusement time is tremendous and can uphold numerous administrations",* it notes.

"Amusement administrations are regularly corresponding, given their extraordinary substance contributions. We accept this is to a great extent why both we and Hulu have had the option to succeed and develop."

In case you are thinking about getting into the stock market, specialists prompt start cautiously.

Experienced investors Warren Buffett, Mark Cuban and Tony Robbins propose you start with list reserves, which offer low turnover rates, specialist expenses and assessment charges, and vary with the market to take out the danger of picking singular stocks. DQYDJ's stock return mini-computer device, which accumulates its numbers from information stage Quandl, appropriately represents stock parts and special dividends by making an "information structure [that] contains the underlying buy and the value vacillations utilizing stock shutting costs every day," as per the site. "Typical parts and dividend occasions cause us to expand the displayed number of shares held. Invert parts will decrease the quantity of shares held." The outcomes are reserved for as long as multi-week so as not to overpower the information supplier. The adding machine doesn't account stock side projects. And keeping in mind that it has a reinvestment device, Netflix's end number, above, doesn't represent reinvestments.

CHAPTER 8

Index and Mutual Funds: Why Not?

An index fund is a group of securities that track the performance of an index. A mutual fund is a professionally managed investment company that pools money from many investors and invests it according to a specific strategy, objective or theme.

A mutual fund may invest in stocks, bonds, money market securities and other investments. An index fund generally tries to match the performance of its benchmark indexes such as the S&P 500 Index or Wilshire 5000 Index which means investing in all stocks in these indices to replicate their composition and return. By investing in all the companies within the index, an index fund takes advantage of diversification which reduces risk and increases return.

Both mutual funds and index funds are managed investment vehicles. Both types of funds offer investors a convenient way to pool their money for investing in securities. Mutual funds have professional management while index funds typically do not. Mutual funds are subject to regulatory oversight and must file annual reports with the SEC, provide semi-annual reports to shareholders, file periodic shareholder reports with the SEC, provide audited financial statements every year and more. Mutual fund shares can only be purchased through a financial professional or an online broker. Index funds can be purchased directly from the fund sponsor without an intermediary, paying a commission.

Both mutual funds and index funds are available as "open-end" investment companies or "closed-end" investment companies. Open-end investment companies add to their capital by continually offering shares to the public for purchase.

Both mutual funds and index funds provide investors with diversification by investing in hundreds or thousands of securities within their respective indices or asset categories. A mutual fund may offer exposure to securities from all over the world or in specific areas such as technology, healthcare, energy and more. An index fund typically does not have the ability to invest in securities outside of its specific index. This limits the risks and rewards experienced by investors.

Mutual funds and index funds are both very tax efficient. Both types of investments may generate capital gains when securities held within the fund are sold for a profit. Both types of funds can benefit from lower taxes by holding their investments within tax-advantaged accounts while waiting to sell other holdings or when redeeming shares into cash (see Taxes on Mutual Funds).

No-load mutual funds do not charge an up-front commission when shares are purchased directly from the fund company or through an online broker (see No-load Fund). Some mutual funds charge a deferred sales charge if shares are redeemed within a certain period after the purchase date (see Load Fund).

Both open-end mutual funds and closed-end index funds can be traded on an exchange at any time. Index funds within the same group (e.g., Vanguard 500 Index Fund, Vanguard Mid-Cap Index Fund) may be bought and sold at any time even though they have different net asset values (NAVs). Most mutual fund families allocate shares to investors on a pro-rata basis each day based on the investor's account balance. The number of index funds available is much larger than the number available for mutual funds. In addition to specialized indexes such as an international index or a small-cap index there are more general-purpose broad market indexes such as the Russell 2000,

S&P 500, Wilshire 5000 and Dow Jones Industrial Average. All of these indexes are tracked by corresponding mutual funds. The size and scope of these indices continually change and it is not uncommon for several new index funds to be launched while other existing index funds are closed or merged with other related index funds.

In theory, stock and bond market exchange prices can move faster than an individual investor's ability to execute transactions over multiple security types within a portfolio. For instance, an investor may wish to sell some bonds and purchase more stocks based upon a change in market conditions. With a mutual fund, investors can accomplish this by selling the bonds and buying the new stocks with a single transaction rather than selling one security then purchasing another separately. The individual investor can use an index fund alone or in combination with other investment strategies such as stock investing, bond investing and money market investing.

Index Fund Investing is the practice of utilizing index funds to build a diversified portfolio of securities for investment purposes.

Because no active (human) decision-making is involved in maintaining the portfolio, costs are low relative to actively managed funds. Actively managed funds depend on a manager to make buying and selling decisions in an attempt to outperform their chosen benchmark index. This can be costly, as the fund manager receives a percentage of asset under management each year. For example, an actively managed fund might charge a 1.5% annual management fee whereas an index fund may charge close to or less than .20%, and some indices like the S&P 500 are even free to invest in passively. In addition, there is still the cost of trading which will come out of your pocket every time you buy or sell a security in your portfolio.

Another cost associated with actively managed mutual funds is the Bid-ask spread. This is the amount of money it costs to get in and out of a position quickly. An index fund has no management to make buying or selling decisions so there aren't any trading costs associated. The Bid-ask spread varies across investment products and markets, but an average study found that this spread averaged between 1/2% to 1% per trade, meaning it costs more to trade with an actively managed mutual fund than an index fund.

An index fund investor doesn't have to worry about what the stock market will do; the indices or indexes they're investing in are designed to track the overall performance of an index like the S&P 500 or various sectors of the economy. The investor also doesn't have to worry about picking stocks or companies that may be losing money. The value of an index fund's investment is based on the value of all the holdings in that index, so if a company loses money, it won't affect your portfolio's performance. If you have a need to invest in the stock market but do not feel comfortable picking stocks or trading options, then there is no better way to invest than via mutual funds.

In order to buy and sell index funds or mutual funds it does require that you have an account with a broker such as TD Ameritrade, TD Trade King, E*Trade, Scottrade and so on. Mutual fund investing is best for beginners who don't want to worry about economic events that affect stocks and might lose money if they became emotional during times like these. Buying into mutual funds is great for many investors to start off with because if they don't have time to do the research and buy stocks then investing in mutual funds can diversify their portfolio of stocks and help them feel more comfortable.

When buying an index fund or a mutual fund there are three different types to choose from.

- The first type is called an "*open-ended*" fund which means that anyone can buy and sell at any time during the day however those who buy or sell on the open market will not receive as favorable of a price as those who invest directly from the company's website.

- The second type is called a *"closed-ended"* fund which means that they only offer a limited number of shares. Once these shares have sold, which can take days or even weeks, the fund will no longer allow anyone to buy into it.
- The third and best way to buy an index fund or mutual fund is called a *"no-load"* fund. A no-load fund is exactly what it says, you will NEVER pay any fees in order to invest in this specific mutual fund. Those who invest in a no-load index fund or mutual fund will receive the same price that the company receives for selling shares.

One very important thing to realize is that it takes money to make money. It doesn't make any sense to buy an index fund and hold onto it for ten years if you are not going to reinvest any of the gains from your initial investment into more shares of the same mutual fund. Therefore, it is a good idea to invest enough money in an index fund or mutual fund so that you can purchase additional shares every time you have excess capital since no one can predict what the stock market will do over a long period of time.

There are different types of index funds and mutual funds to invest in:

- The first type is called an *"Index Fund"* which tracks an index such as the S&P 500, Dow Jones 30 Industrial Average or the NASDAQ Composite. These funds will hold every single stock that is in the index which means that it diversifies your holdings by spreading your money across thousands of stocks. This is one of the most important factors of a mutual fund because just because one stock performed poorly over a period of time does not mean that every other stock in the index fund will do poorly as well. Therefore, since you are diversifying your holdings by buying thousands of different stocks with just a couple hundred dollars you will experience less volatility in your portfolio.

- The second type of mutual fund is called a *"Dividend Income Fund"*. These funds will invest in dividend-paying stocks such as those which pay dividends in order to provide their investors with income. Usually these funds will have a large portion of their holdings in utility companies, real estate companies and even some healthcare stocks.
- The third type of mutual fund is called an *"Active Management Fund"* which means that the manager of the fund can make different types of investments other than buying all of the stocks in the index. The active management fund can also buy bonds, foreign currencies or even commodities within your portfolio.

The last type of mutual fund is called a "Fund of Funds" which means that it contains different types of mutual funds. When investing in a fund of funds you should look for one that has several different types of funds so that your money is protected against poor performance in one specific fund or index.

Once you have decided to invest in an index fund or mutual fund then the easiest way to purchase shares would be through the company directly since they will charge you less fees. However, if you don't have enough money to make a direct investment then there is another way to invest. You can always start with a small amount of money and then reinvest the gains from your initial investment in the same mutual fund.

If you are just starting out in the stock market it is important that you do not buy an index fund or mutual fund without knowing what it does. Every mutual fund will usually have a prospectus which explains everything about that specific index fund or mutual fund. If there are any questions about the fund, then you should follow up with a phone call to the company.

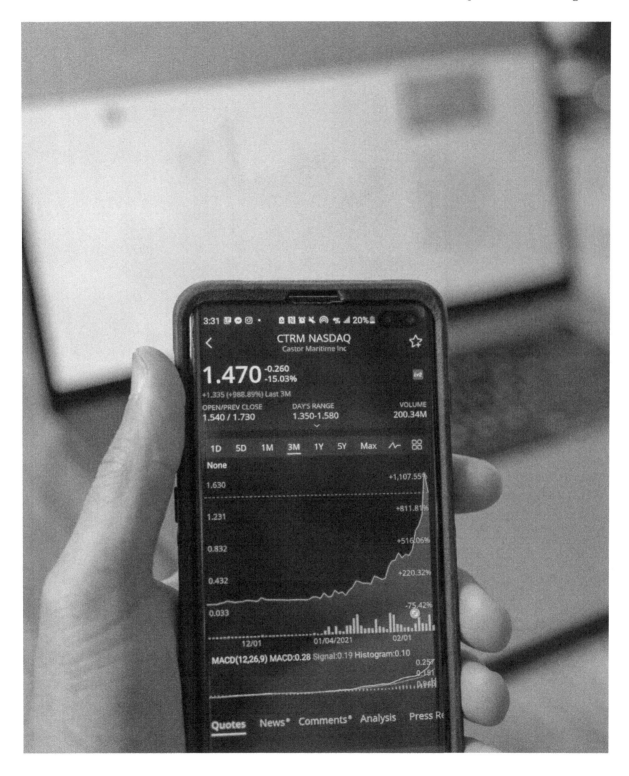

Warren Miller

CHAPTER 9

Exchange-Traded Funds (ETFs)

There has been a lot of buzz around ETFs in the media lately. You may have read, for instance, that they can offer diversification and lower costs. And that's true—but it's not the whole story! ETFs are investment funds that track an index, commodity or other benchmark. They trade like stocks on an exchange and seek to match their performance without any added management fees-making them a great option for individual investors who want to minimize trading costs. But similar to most investment vehicles, ETFs have some unique pros and cons. Here's what investors should know to make educated decisions about whether these funds are right for them.

What Makes an ETF Different?

ETFs are not mutual funds or other types of managed products such as exchange-traded notes (ETNs). They are structured to track a particular investment benchmark instead of seeking to outperform it. For example, an ETF may hold stocks or bonds that are included in the S&P 500 index. Another way to think about it is that benchmarks usually represent a diversified basket of securities within a particular category and are generally calculated and maintained by third parties such as an index provider (e.g. MSCI, the Federal Reserve, etc.)

For example: an ETF might hold a handful of stocks it believes to be representative of the S&P 500 index, or even all 500 stocks. It only seeks to match what the index has done during the prior trading day by providing investors with an intraday return equal to that of the benchmark on a given day.

So, What's in an ETF?

ETFs are generally structured as Unit Investment Trusts (UITs), which means they're open-ended and ongoing vehicles that issue redeemable shares. They can invest in anything from equities and bonds to metals and commodities. They are also passively managed and their portfolios are valued daily because they're traded on an exchange. Some ETFs even provide the ability to short specific securities or indexes, giving investors more flexibility. Exchange-Traded Funds are a type of mutual fund that can be traded like stocks. It is an investment that provides diversified exposure to assets such as stocks, bonds, or commodities. There are many ETFs and they come in different shapes and sizes with various strategies, which means it may take some time to figure out what you're looking for.

Here we are going to discuss different types of Exchange-Traded Funds to give you a general idea of what they are and why you might use them.

Index ETFs

Index ETFs passively track an underlying index. For example, the Standard and Poor's 500 Index, which is comprised of the largest companies in the US market by market capitalization listed on the NYSE or NASDAQ. When you invest in an index ETF, you are investing in a basket of securities representing that particular index. Therefore, if your investment goes up then it's because your underlying basket did well too whether it's based on investable indexes such as bond indexes or non-investable indexes such as commodity indexes.

ETFs That Aim to Track a Specific Index and Outperform It

These ETFs hold the underlying securities in the same proportion as they appear in the index, but they are designed to outperform it. This means that if, for example, you're expecting a large capital gain in a particular sector then you'd want to buy an ETF that aims to track the benchmark but with less volatility. For example, you might invest in an ETF that tracks the S&P 500 Index but invests 75% of its holdings in stocks with above-average fundamentals such as high earnings growth and low debt.

Sector Funds — US-Based Indexes

These aim to track a specific sector such as technology or health care. If you are looking to invest in a specific sector, then you might want to consider an ETF that bets on one of these sectors.

Broadly Diversified ETFs

These are similar to index ETFs and hold a basket of assets and track the index but have a broader spectrum of holdings. While this means more diversification, it also means less individual stock research is required. An investor who does not want to spend much time monitoring his investments may prefer this type of fund.

Managed ETFs

These are actively managed ETFs. They require the work of an investment manager to oversee their holdings and are not tied to a particular index.

In summary, if you're looking for a simple way to invest in stocks and bonds then consider using an ETF; however, be sure to do your research before making any final decisions about which type of ETF is right for you and, perhaps more importantly, how to buy them. As the number of Exchange-Traded Funds increases so does the number of ways for investors to trade them, including direct access trading as well as traditional brokers and advisors.

It is also possible to trade an ETF in a tax-advantaged account such as a 401(k) or an IRA (using a Traditional or Roth IRA). This may allow for some tax advantages that would be unavailable from using other investment vehicles.

Apart from the bid-ask spread, investors should consider brokerage and transfer fees, which can vary depending on the selected trading platform. In addition, additional fees may apply when investing in specific ETFs. For example, some types of ETFs have higher per-trade commissions than others.

In addition, if an investor plans to trade frequently or reinvest his dividends (a common strategy) he could incur significant transaction costs in a short period if he chooses to use a brokerage firm that offers low trading commissions for individual trades.

ETFs can be held alongside other investments such as mutual funds or stocks. This makes them useful in constructing a well-rounded portfolio that offers diversification and liquidity to investors. However, not all ETFs can be freely bought and sold in an investor's brokerage account. Those that are listed on exchanges must meet certain requirements and therefore have more liquidity than others, which may only be available to trade via order book at major brokerage houses (for example, Guggenheim S&P 500 Equal Weight ETF (RSP)).

Other widely traded U.S. ETFs include the iShares Core S&P Mid-Cap ETF (IJH), which tracks the S&P MidCap 400 index, and the iShares Russell 2000 ETF (IWM), which tracks the Russell 2000 Index.

ETFs may appeal to certain investors who want to invest in a specific sector or country, but lack sufficient capital or time to build a portfolio of individual securities. By using an ETF, an investor can quickly assemble a diverse basket of securities that track specific markets such as oil and gas drilling companies or an entire nation's stock market.

Now let us explore when one should buy and sell Exchange-Traded Funds (ETFs).

ETFs have been around for almost two decades and they are quickly becoming mainstream. In fact, ETFs now represent one of the most important financial investment products in the marketplace. Some investors use ETFs as a way to gain exposure to different securities such as commodities, stocks or bonds—all with just one trade. An investor may want exposure to a particular industry sector but does not want the risk that comes with individual stock ownership. The investor can purchase an index-based ETF that tracks a specific group of securities providing diversification benefits in this manner. While there are many different ETFs out there, they can be grouped into three main categories: Equity ETFs; Fixed Income ETFs; Commodity ETFs. Within each of these categories are numerous sub-categories.

Here is a sampling:

Equity ETFs

- Global Equity (including emerging markets)

- Large Cap Value (e.g., iShares S&P 500 Value Index Fund)

- Mid Cap (e.g., iShares S&P MidCap Index Fund)

- Small Cap (e.g., iShares Russell 2000 Index Fund)

- Industrials (e.g. Power Shares Dynamic Industrials Portfolio)

- Real Estate (e.g., Market Vectors Retail REIT ETF)

Fixed Income ETFs

- US treasury (e.g., iShares iBoxx T-Bond Index Fund) — This is a good way to play the changing interest rate environment.

- High Yield (e.g., Direxion Daily 20+ Year Treasury Bear 3X Shares) — This is a good way to play the credit markets including financial stocks.

- Municipal Bonds (e.g. iShares S&P National AMT-Free Muni Bond Index Fund) — This is a good way to play the municipal bond market.

Commodity ETFs

- Energy (e.g., Market Vectors Oil Refiners ETF) — This is a good way to play the energy sector.

- Precious Metals (e.g., SPDR Gold Shares) — This is a good way to play the precious metal sector.

- Agriculture (e.g., Power Shares DB Agriculture Fund) — This is a good way to play the agriculture sector.

As one can see, ETFs can be used in numerous ways for a variety of purposes. The question is: When should one buy or sell an ETF? The general consensus is that if an individual investor would like to invest in the stock market but does not want to actually buy and sell stocks outright, then an ETF product may be the right investment vehicle. Likewise, if someone wants exposure to commodities—but does not want to actually buy and sell physical gold, silver or soybeans—then a commodity ETF will provide this type of exposure. If you are buying a particular ETF for the long-term and mean to keep it there until you need your money, then you can hold on until retirement. On the other hand, if you plan to trade more actively and have the time to do so, then there may be times when you should buy and sell ETFs. For example, if stock markets enter a prolonged down cycle, an investor may decide to get out there and buy stocks at these lower levels after a correction in order to replace those stocks that are now underperforming their benchmarks. At such a time, selling their ETF shares and buying individual stocks would provide this type of exposure. There was one particular individual who bought shares in a small-cap value ETF against the advice of many Wall Street professionals. He held his position during the 2008 market crash and today is one of the most over-leveraged, but also one of the most profitable investors out there. Conversely, if markets are going up for an extended period of time as they have been in recent years, an ETF investor may decide to get out there and sell their holdings in order to take profits. Again, selling their shares and buying individual stocks would provide such exposure. In recent years, we have seen many investors who sold their holdings of small-cap value ETFs in order to buy large-cap value stocks (e.g., iShares Russell 2000 Value Index Fund vs iShares S&P 500 Value Index Fund). While this strategy is a great way to hedge one's bet, it is not advisable to make such drastic changes all at once. While there are several risks and complexities associated with investing in ETFs, individuals who take the time to educate themselves on what they are buying should be able to avoid some of the pitfalls. What is important is that investors in ETFs remember that these investments are not immune to extreme downward changes just because they may have done well over the long term.

Warren Miller

CHAPTER 10

Other Types of Investments

Cryptocurrencies

Cryptocurrencies are a medium of exchange using cryptography to secure transactions, control the creation of additional units, and authenticate the transfer of assets. Cryptocurrencies let buyers and sellers conduct financial transactions without revealing their identities. By decentralizing public transaction data, cryptocurrencies eliminate the need for third-party checking and verification. The first cryptocurrency to capture popular attention was Bitcoin, which was launched in 2009 by an individual or group operating under the name Satoshi Nakamoto. Like other currencies, Bitcoins are not backed by a physical commodity but rather by a peer-to-peer network of computers users who use the coins as money.

What Is Bitcoin?

Bitcoin was introduced on 31 October 2008 to a cryptography mailing list, and released as open-source software in 2009. It is a cryptocurrency, so-called because it uses cryptography to control the creation of its units of currency and verify the transfer of assets. Bitcoin transactions are irreversible and immune to fraudulent chargebacks. The system is peer-to-peer and transactions take place between users directly through the use of cryptography.

If you are looking for the top places to buy and sell Cryptocurrencies, this article provides a list of the best cryptocurrency exchanges. The Bitcoin market is an important space that has been sending traders scrambling in search of a reliable exchange platform. If you want to invest in cryptocurrencies, then there are five exchanges on which you can do so: Coinbase, Bit stamp, Kraken, Bitfinex and Poloniex.

You may not be familiar with all of these platforms as they tend to cater to more tech-savvy traders. What's interesting about each is that they vary in their approach to how you buy and sell cryptocurrencies—in other words what currencies they offer and how advanced their trading infrastructure is.

Gold and Silver

Investing in physical gold and silver is a tangible, proven strategy to hedge against economic uncertainty. It cannot be stolen like the cash in your bank account, and it doesn't need an internet connection to retain its value. Gold and silver are liquid assets that can be conveniently transformed into cash at any time, with no restrictive holding periods or costs. Many people put off purchasing physical gold or silver because they feel it's a complicated process that requires significant research or expertise, but the truth is that you don't need any special skills or training to get started investing in physical gold and silver.

Gold is primarily an investment whereas silver is primarily industrial. Quite simply, gold has a far greater store of value as a raw commodity than silver does. However, because it is primarily an investment rather than an industrial metal, it can experience swings in price more dramatically than the price fluctuations experienced by silver, which is used more for practical purposes such as jewelry or in medicine.

Precious metals purchased through your brokerage account with a bank or credit union may be covered by the Federal Deposit Insurance Corp., but check with the company first. Insurance payouts can take up to 60 days; the metal itself is typically received in three days.

Private Equity

Private equity has been around since the 1970s, but for some reason these days it is getting a lot of attention. Private equity is a type of investment fund that uses investors' money to buy companies.

It can seem intimidating to figure out when and where to buy and sell private equity — but if you are looking to make some money, this post will bring you up-to-speed on the basics and help you get started.

Private equity is a straightforward concept.

A private equity fund is almost exactly the same as any other investment fund (like a mutual fund or hedge fund)—it just invests in a slightly different type of investment.

As with other types of funds, private equity funds will be bought and sold on stock exchanges. You can use exchange-traded funds (ETFs) to invest in large private equity firms like Blackstone and TPG Capital. For traders, the ETFs for Blackstone and TPG Capital are BXLT and TPLM, respectively.

If you are looking to buy individual stocks, you can look into stocks of smaller companies that are held by private equity firms. For example, Marriott, Hyatt and Hilton are all owned by private equity firms like Blackstone.

The biggest drawback to private equity investing is that it is a lot riskier. If you are invested in a mutual fund that owns stock, the worst-case scenario is a complete loss of your investment—but this would be extremely rare because most companies do not go completely bankrupt.

In contrast, private equity funds can lose all of their money and often times will.

And even though private equity funds are a type of investment fund and have the same risk/reward characteristic as other types of investment funds, they are taxed differently.

Rather than being taxed only when you sell your investment (like mutual funds), private equity is taxed on a yearly basis—the amount invested plus profit is considered income each year.

Hedge Funds

Hedge funds is an industry that deals in the regulation of investments and speculation. The hedge fund industry has experienced significant growth in recent years, with over 8,000 hedge funds managing about $3 trillion in assets as of December 2013. This article aims to provide a brief overview of the historical background, descriptions, advantages and disadvantages of hedge funds as well as the potential risks involved with this type of investment vehicles. Hedge Funds, or funds of hedge funds, are investment vehicles that are made out of investments in other investment companies. The most common form of a hedge fund is a pooled investment vehicle with the goal to reduce risk by using an array of investments and trading strategies. Hedge funds have been used since 1954 and were created because conventional publicly traded securities were producing less than satisfactory returns. The goal is to make as much money as possible while also ensuring that the investor does not lose any money on bad trades. A hedge fund manager is a person who earns money via performance fees, incentive compensation, and trading profits.

Ethical Investments

Ethical investing is a technique where an investor picks investment dependent on an individual ethical code. Ethical investing endeavors to help enterprises having a constructive outcome, for example, manageable energy, and make an investment return. With an increment in ESG assets, there are more ethical investments than any other time in recent memory. Obviously, what is "ethical" relies upon the individual. What is ethical to you may not be to another person. That is the reason it is essential to look in the background of ethical investments and ensure they line up with the effect you would prefer to have. While no investment is ensured, the exhibition of ethical assets has been demonstrated to be like the presentation of customary assets—truth be told, some exploration shows that ethical asset execution might be predominant. As indicated by Morningstar information, maintainable assets beat their conventional friends in 2019, with 66% completing the year with returns in the top portion of their Morningstar classes. There is likewise some proof that recommends that ethical assets may offer lower levels of market hazard than customary assets, even in unstable markets, for example, the plunge during the initial many months of the COVID-19 pandemic. As indicated by Morningstar information, 24 out of 26 ESG list supports outflanked tantamount ordinary assets during the main quarter of 2020.

Coins, Stamps and Art

Coins

Coins are well-known investments, but they can often be hard to come by. One of the most popular ones for collectors are US pennies before the year 1982. Most will start at about $5 and increase at about 10% per year—depending on the date you buy one and when you sell it. Most people don't keep track of coins for their entire life, so when they're found in old furniture or wallets, the owner will sell them to a coin collector.

Stamps

Stamps are another collectible. They aren't as popular as coins or other collectibles because they're fairly easy to find, but for stamps issued after 1989 (when they stopped using the mail system to sell them), you can expect an increase in value of about 10% per year.

Art

If you are in the mood to invest in something more artistic, then art might be just the thing. The timelessness of great works of art is legendary, so the investment potential is gigantic. There are other reasons to invest in art, too. For example, if your home or office has a limited amount of wall space, buying an art piece will add value to the environment—and if you are not able to repay your loan on the art, then you can just sell it again later and recoup some of your losses. Are you looking for ways to invest your money? Coins, stamps and art are three ways to consider. Collectible coins can be a solid investment when done strategically. Stamps can also provide an interesting opportunity if you know how to buy and sell them effectively. Finally, art has always been viewed as one of the most lucrative investments out there, though many people don't see it as a realistic option for their budgets.

The Purchase of Comic Books

Comic books are exciting and fun. They bring out the imagination, and some of them even have their own movie. Interestingly enough, most people who read them know little about the process of producing comic books these days. Though they remain popular, the industry itself is not as lucrative as it was in years past. The irony is that people will continue to buy comics whether they are produced by Marvel or DC Comics or some other company. They are an industry investment that can result in nice profits depending on how long you hold onto them.

There is a tremendous amount of risk involved with buying comic books for investment purposes because they can be lost easily. You may have had this happen to you or someone you know in the past. They go into storage for years and get damaged or destroyed completely. You don't want this to happen with your comic books because of the money that is tied up in them and their future potential value.

One of the best ways to invest in comic books without having to worry about storage is through one of the current comic book dealers on the market who takes care of storing your comic books for a monthly fee, rather than having you store them yourself. You will not have to worry about collecting them anymore, and it also ensures that they will not be lost forever.

Warren Miller

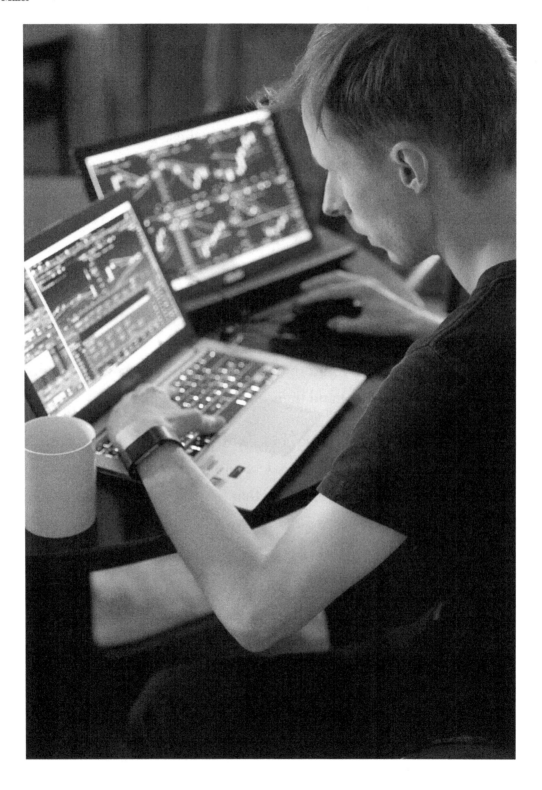

CHAPTER 11

How to Manage Your Investment Portfolio

Managing an investment portfolio is an important skill for any young investor to learn. The main reason is that, as you get older, you will be able to acquire more capital to invest. Investing during your teen years will provide you with the opportunity to learn important skills that you can use when managing your own investment portfolio later in life.

To get started, let's start by examining the basics of what an investment portfolio is, and what it takes to manage one successfully. Then we can look at how these skills can be acquired by a young investor like yourself.

What Is an Investment Portfolio?

An investment portfolio is basically everything that you own that has value (either tangible or intangible). For example, if you owned a car it would be part of your investment portfolio. If you owned a $100 bill, that would also be part of your investment portfolio. Even if you have no money invested yet, the time that you spend working on your education (and the knowledge that results) is also an investment and therefore part of an investment portfolio. The recent bear market has shaken many investors' confidence. Having lived through the previous bear market from 1973 to 1974, there are some investors who are perhaps feeling a bit anxious about how they will handle a similar scenario in the future. In this section, we will look at how management of your portfolio can help you manage your nerves during periods of market volatility. There are two basic ways to manage an investment portfolio: (1) You can stay invested no matter what happens in the market, or (2) you can time your moves based on market conditions and try to capture gains when you think a rally is coming. Let's take a look at these two strategies and see which may work best for you.

Strategy #1: Stay Invested All the Time

This strategy suggests that investors stay invested all the time, and worry only about managing their portfolio with new contributions and rebalancing their holdings periodically. This is probably the more passive approach, and doesn't require you to read The Wall Street Journal every day. It also helps remove some of the emotion from investing decisions. The idea is that over the long term, if you hold a diversified portfolio of stocks, bonds, and cash equivalents (T-Bills), your investments will behave in a predictable manner, allowing you to ignore daily market fluctuations. You just check how your investments are doing every once in a while.

The major drawback to this approach is that you will have to weather some very difficult periods. For example, consider the year 2000 when the NASDAQ plunged nearly 50% in just over a year. A portfolio in just the S&P 500 Index would have dropped about 30% during that same period. If you were holding all your investments in stocks at that time, it would have been very difficult to stick with your plan and stay invested all the way through until 2002.

Strategy #2: Try to Time the Market

The second strategy is to try and time the market. This approach involves having a well-developed understanding of current economic conditions, an understanding of how these conditions are impacting the markets, and then making your buying and selling decisions based on that knowledge. The basic idea is that if you can figure out the best times to buy and sell, you will be able to outperform the market over time.

In order to implement this strategy successfully, you need considerable expertise in financial analysis. You also need a lot of patience because short-term results will vary significantly with each decision on when to buy or sell. For example, let's assume that you had correctly guessed that the stock market was going to start recovering in April 2003. You could then have liquidated your stocks and invested in a short-term government bond fund. In April 2003, the Vanguard Short-Term Government Bond Index Fund (NYSE: VFSUX) yielded 3.01%, which was significantly better than the 2.37% you would have earned from an S&P 500 index fund during that same period. The problem with this type of move is that if you were wrong about rising stocks, then you would have paid a big price for your mistake. For example, if you had sold your stocks and invested in the bond fund in April 2002, you would have lost about 7% over the next 10 months.

As you can see, there is a very fine line between successfully timing the market and simply guessing wrong. To succeed at this game over time requires a huge amount of knowledge about economic conditions and market trends, as well as a tolerance for short-term losses when you are wrong. Even then, trying to time the market isn't for everybody. It is a very challenging approach that requires a lot of effort.

So which approach is best? The answer depends on your personality type. If you have the ability to read the market and understand how current economic conditions will impact your investments, then timing the market will give you a better chance of long-term success. If that is too difficult for you, then sticking with your long-term plan and just checking in from time to time might be a better way to go.

Warren Miller

CHAPTER 12

Personal Advisor and Online Brokers

Your financial security is important. However, for some of us, it can be an area we find difficult to understand and manage. That's why so many of us turn to an advisor—someone who has experience in these areas and can help you make decisions that will keep your finances on the right track. So what are your options?

A personal advisor is a good option for people who would like one-on-one guidance with their finances. They will typically take a comprehensive approach, looking at all aspects of your financial life from debt to taxes to savings. Personal advisors might charge by the hour or they might have a set monthly fee, depending on their arrangement with you. *Benefits:* A personal advisor will look at your whole financial picture and help you make decisions that are right for your life situation. You will have one primary point person who is available to you and to whom you can build a relationship. *Potential drawbacks:* Personal advisors are often expensive, though they might be willing to offer a free consultation in order to win your business.

An online broker is an automated way to invest that comes with the expertise and industry contacts of an independent investment firm. The internet-based platforms for these types of accounts are easy to use, but they also offer personalized advice from expert analysts who can help you choose the investments that best fit your goals. *Benefits:* Online brokers can be a good option for people who are comfortable doing their own financial research but want help from people with experience. These types of advisors can allow you to invest on your own, but also give you the benefit of a team behind the scenes that can offer advice and answer questions. *Potential drawbacks:* If you are nervous about investing without seeing what you are buying, this is not for you. There is no ability to ask the analyst for advice; an online platform makes recommendations based on your goals and risk tolerance.

Every day, consumers are bombarded with messages from online brokers and advisors. With so many different solutions to choose from, it is hard for people to know which one is best. Additionally, the products they offer are typically not easy to compare because there are no universal standards in the financial industry. This makes selecting an advisor and broker very challenging for people who are new to investing or don't have time to research all the options themselves. Putting together this brief article has thus become a necessity because we understand first-hand how overwhelming this process can be. We've gone through it too, and have put together some helpful tips that make the comparison easier. If you're planning to use any of the services listed in this report, you should pay attention to the following factors:

1) **Education.** The first and most important thing to check is educational background. Does it have any? What are they? These degrees will tell you what kind of investor the advisor is. For example, if it has a finance-related degree, such as MSc in Financial Analysis or Certified Financial Planner, then it can give you an idea of whether it will be able to provide intelligent and relevant advice. For people who want a more personal touch in their lives, such as with health or relationship issues, a Master's degree in psychology or social work may be best for them.

2) **Experience.** The second most important factor is how long has the advisor been in business. You want someone who has been established and remained relevant for at least a few years, because this shows it has survived and grown based on the quality of service it provides.

3) **Licenses and Insurance.** Brokers can be certified by organizations such as Chartered Financial Analyst (CFA), Certified Financial Planner (CFP), Chartered Life Underwriter (CLU), Chartered Life Specialist (CLS) or Registered Investment Advisor (RIA). They ensure that a professional follow certain ethical standard and maintain a proper level of education required to serve you better. Most of the time, these credentials mean the advisor is an experienced professional in the industry. But it doesn't mean they are a good fit for you. They are just a sign that you can trust what they offer because these licenses have qualifications that can only be gained through meaningful coursework and relevant experience.

   It is also important to double-check that your advisors carry liability insurance and fidelity bond, which protect you if something goes wrong. The reason you need to be cautious about this is because there are some dishonest individuals in the financial world who may wish to take advantage of unwary customers. The best way to avoid this is to only deal with well-established and reputable brokers.

4) **Tax Filing Services.** Many people do not consider the importance of picking a qualified tax filing service, which is only natural because most of us do not like dealing with numbers, especially when it comes to taxes. But tax filing services are important because they can help make sure you stay on top of your taxes and also ensure that you're not audited by the government for paying too little or too much in taxes. This will save a lot of headaches for you over the years, as running afoul with the IRS can result in a painful consequence if you fail to pay them properly or handle your expenses incorrectly.

5) **Investment Portfolio**. Some brokers are solely online investment platforms and do not offer any other services. On the other hand, some of them manage funds and stocks directly for you as a customer. This requires special licensing

and also brings with its certain risks, so you want to make sure you choose a solution that is most appropriate for your unique needs.

6) **Commissions and Fees.** While the commissions may vary from one broker to another, the main thing you need to look at is whether or not they charge fees on top of their commissions. This can be quite costly over time because it can add up exponentially if you do not check or evaluate your portfolio often enough. This is why it's better to go with a broker that only charges commissions, which will not cost you anything else.

7) **Brokerage Accounts and Products.** As for the products they offer, many brokers have low or no-minimum requirements, which is great because it ensures more people can get into the market without having to make a large upfront investment.

8) **Customer Service.** Lastly, do they have good customer service? All companies offer some form of customer support these days, but some of these are just unaccountably bad—so much so that it seems like they do not care about their clients at all. This is why you should really make sure the company you're dealing with has good customer service, which should be both prompt and thorough.

A good broker will not just find you the right financial products to invest in, but will also help you monitor your investment portfolio as well as provide education every step of the way. This will ensure that your investments grow steadily and without any undue risk. The end goal is to have a steady stream of passive income for retirement that allows you to comfortably live out the last years of your life in peace and happiness.

How to Open a Broker Account

Opening a broker account is very simple; all you need to provide is basic information (name and address) and then deposit money into the account so that you are able to start trading with real money on the market.

You'll need to provide your social security number (or your tax id) and agree to the terms of service. After filling that out, you'll be brought to a page that asks for your financial account information.

Make sure you only put in information for whatever bank or brokerage account you want to deposit money into! After completing these steps, check your email to confirm your Account information. Finally, you'll get into page where you will be able to deposit money into your brokerage account.

I recommend depositing $500 or more but at least $100 so that you are able to start trading on the market. This is an easy way for us introduce you to investing with a Broker Account. You can read through the rest of websites to learn more about it if you want.

Warren Miller

CHAPTER 13

Best Investing and Micro-Savings Apps

The world is changing. People are working more and more hours on two jobs. There is less time to do things that you enjoy and too much work to do in your spare time. Many people have no choice but to work hard for the money, but there is still a choice about how you invest that money, which can make all the difference in your future financial health.

Investing Vs Micro-Savings Apps

We have been taught that the stock market is how you make money. However, it has become increasingly difficult to access stock market investments and sometimes even to understand them. The methods that used to work aren't as reliable as they used to be, and investing in individual stocks can be risky.

The other alternative is micro-savings apps—which in our opinion are less work, more convenient and more secure than stock trading/investing. They also have the potential for being much more profitable in the long-term because of their compound interest rate multipliers built in. This means your money really grows on itself and the more it makes, the more it can make. This is as opposed to stock market investments in which you must wait for a company to pay out dividends (if they do) or sell your stock at a profit. In addition, micro-savings apps can be used and accessed from anywhere in the world with an internet connection, so you can invest your money from anywhere without having to deal with geographical restrictions.

The Best Micro-Savings Apps

We have chosen these apps by considering budget, time available to make money, acquired financial experience and of course their potential return on investment.

1. Acorns

With Acorns, you can invest your money as frequently as you want and have it automatically withdrawn from your debit card or bank account.

The Acorns "Roundup" feature allows customers to make micro-savings for free each time they shop at a retailer with a supported credit or debit card, without changing their shopping habits. Whenever a purchase is made, the app rounds up to the nearest dollar and invests the remaining change into an Acorns portfolio.

Acorns have also partnered with influential business leaders such as Yahoo CEO Marissa Mayer and Uber board member Bill Gurley to offer challenges that can earn its users additional cash rewards for investing early, often, and responsibly.

Additionally, the app has an easy-to-understand and user-friendly interface that makes it accessible to new investors.

The only drawback is fees—Acorns charges $1 a month for balances under $5,000 (or 0.25% of assets per year); $2 a month for balances above that threshold (or 0.25%). You can also try out Acorns' free version for 14 days.

2. Stash

Stash's goal is to make investing simple and cost-effective. The app serves as a platform for every type of investment from trading stocks, to spending your spare change. Unlike other apps on the market, Stash offers customers the ability to choose how they want to invest their money—by selecting an area of personal interest like "politics" or "sports".

If you are not sure where to start, the app will also suggest a portfolio based on your age and financial goals. Initially launched in 2015, Stash has gone through several iterations in terms of features and functionality with its newest release in March 2017.

The current version of the app allows users to:

- Invest as little as $5 at a time across hundreds of different investments (no minimum balance requirement).

- Decide how they wish to be billed (quarterly, monthly and yearly).

- Link up a bank account or debit card for easy and convenient automated investing.

- Choose from hundreds of stocks, bonds, ETFs, and cryptocurrencies.

Recent updates to the app include "Watch-lists"—which allow users to track relevant stocks and cryptocurrencies in real-time. Stash also offers educational tools like "Stash Academy"—a personal finance library with articles related to money management. For those who want more information about the principles behind investing their money, "Stash University" is an interactive investing course that walks users through key concepts like diversification and risk tolerance.

3. Acorns Spend

Acorns recently launched Acorns Spend, a free app that is similar to the original app, but instead of investing your money, you can save it with it. Though the two apps have similarities—like round-up and invest features and checklists—they differ in the fact that Acorns Spend allows customers to spend their spare change without having to make adjustments to their financial habits. With a linked debit or credit card, Acorns Spend round up your purchases like Acorns and invests the change using the same investment portfolio found in its other app, while also eating into your debit or credit card's budget. What sets this app apart from the competition is its generous savings potential—users can save up to 5.4% or $1,215 a year for someone making $50,000 annually—based on the app's tax efficiency algorithm. The algorithm works by identifying financial opportunities and effectively minimizing your tax obligations by maximizing your pre-tax dollars. Another feature that sets Acorns Spend apart from other apps of its kind is the fact that it allows customers to spend their money in real-time without any account minimums or monthly fees for balances under $5,000 (or 0.25% of assets per year). However, if users are looking to invest their savings instead of spending them, they will have to upgrade to the regular Acorns or Acorns Later app.

4. Tiller

Tiller provides a service called "Bill Paying Made Simple". According to the company's website:

"Tiller is a smart, easy to use personal finance manager that gives you the tools to better understand and manage your money. With Tiller, you can quickly see where your money is going and take control without spending tons of time analyzing spreadsheets or inputting data."

Here's how it works: Customers pay certain bills from their checking accounts (i.e. rent, credit cards bills, car loans, etc.) through their Tiller account for free with no fees. There are different tiers of service offered by Tiller depending on what you pay them each month. For example, the most basic level of service costs $2.50 per month for customers who pay an average of $500 per month in bills through the service. The second-tier costs $4.95 a month for customers with monthly payments totaling more than $1,000. The third level charges 5.95 monthly for those who pay more than $5,000 in bills a month through the service. Using Tiller to pay bills can save you money.

It might not seem like paying a few bucks to save yourself hours of work is worth it but when you consider all the time you'll save over your lifetime on tedious tasks, it is well worth it. The company is also taking longer to achieve profit-making status. In 1998 and 1999, 89% of the companies funded by venture capitalists went public or were acquired within 4 years. This year, the figure was 64%.

The shift from initial public offerings to mergers may reflect an increase in Internet companies that are not yet profitable but have strong brand names and sites with loyal users. For example, Amazon.com Inc. was able to raise $54 million in its 1997 initial public offering, but it had annual losses of about $500,000 before it began posting profits.

The company grew quickly and in March 2000, less than a year after going public, Amazon agreed to be acquired by online bookseller Barnes & Noble for $1.45 billion.

"We're in the second wave of venture-capital investing," says Michael Sinkin, who runs Red Mile Group Inc., an e-commerce consulting firm in New York. *"It's much more likely now that venture capitalists will make money through an acquisition. It's harder to make money through an IPO."*

The second wave may last longer, too. *"In the 1990s,"* says Mr. Sinkin, *"I'd see venture capitalists get excited about a new idea and try it out. If it didn't work, they'd fold up and move on to something else."* Now that e-commerce and e-business are mature industries, people expect to spend years working on them. There is little doubt that the venture capitalists will be along for the ride.

In the meantime, they are making money from companies like Tiller. The company charges a monthly fee of $2.50 to $5.95 for its services, but the savings can far outweigh the costs. For example, instead of letting your landlord collect your rent on a monthly basis by sending you a check or charging it to your credit card, you can have all of your rent automatically withdrawn from your checking account and sent directly to him or her—and save yourself the transaction fee and the time spent writing out checks. Here is how it works: You can use Tiller to pay all federal bills that charge a flat fee plus postage (such as income tax payments). You can also ask any company that sends invoices to you (such as your cable-TV provider) whether it will accept payments through Tiller. Once you have set up a biller on Tiller, you can pay your bills right through your bank account.

5. Robinhood Financial (Formerly "Robinhood")

The Robinhood app, which lets users to trade U.S. stocks for free, provides an easy-to-use platform that can help anyone learn the basics of investing in the stock market and save money on commissions.

The app is fairly intuitive—users can tap on a company's name to see how it's performing or tap on the menu icon to view all available stocks and options and their respective prices in real-time (unlike other apps that only provide stock information).

6. M1 Finance

Founded in 2014 by Alex Friedman and Jacob Gibson, M1 Finance is a free mobile app that allows customers to manage and invest their money. Similar to Robinhood, M1 offers commission-free trading on thousands of ETFs and stocks with no minimum account balance required.

The app's tax optimization feature helps customers maximize the after-tax growth potential of their investments by identifying cost basis.

Even though it is free to use, M1 charges a fee of $0.0035 for every stock trade and an ETF trading fee of $0.0025 for every share traded.

M1 also offers a "Smart Deposit" feature that automatically invests the money users deposit into their M1 account into their respective investment portfolios. The more money customers deposit into their accounts, the more money they will have in their investment portfolios (up to $15,000). The company offers taxable users two custodial accounts: one with short-term capital gains and one with long-term capital gains.

One drawback for M1 is that users have to manually invest their money, which is an annoyance for those who don't have a solid understanding of investments and trading. Another drawback is that there isn't a mobile-based app to manage accounts from iOS devices. However, M1 does have an iPhone app, but it doesn't look as polished as Robinhood's.

Warren Miller

CHAPTER 14

Mistakes to Avoid

Five Huge Mistakes that Beginners Make

I get many messages each day from merchants and investors, a large number of whom have quite recently committed one of the errors that I talk about in this section. In the event that you can keep away from these slip-ups when you are simply beginning, you will be path in front of the pack and will likewise save yourself a ton of misfortunes and wretchedness.

1. Try not to purchase stocks that are hitting 52-week lows

We have just examined this point, however it bears rehashing, in light of the fact that such countless new brokers lose a ton of cash attempting to get the famous "falling blade". Notwithstanding what everybody will advise you, you are quite often much better purchasing a stock that is hitting 52-week highs than one hitting 52-week lows.

Has an organization that you own just announced some truly downright terrible? Assuming this is the case, recollect that there will never be only one cockroach. Awful news comes in bunches.

Numerous investors as of late scholarly this the most difficult way possible with General Electric, which just continued announcing something terrible after another, making the stock slump from 30 to 7. There is nothing of the sort as a "protected stock". Even a blue-chip stock can go down a great deal on the off chance that it loses its upper hand or the organization settles on awful choices. A course of terrible news can regularly make a stock pattern down or hold down more than once. In the event that you own a stock that does this, it is frequently better to get out and stand by a couple of months (or years) to reappear. Again, there will never be only one cockroach.

2. Try not to exchange penny stocks

A penny stock is any stock that exchanges under $5. Except if you are a high-level broker, you ought to stay away from all penny stocks. I would stretch out this by urging you to likewise evade all stocks estimated under $10.

Regardless of whether you have a little exchanging account ($5,000) or less, you are in an ideal situation purchasing less portions of a more expensive stock than a great deal of portions of a penny stock.

That is on the grounds that low-estimated stocks are frequently connected with lower quality organizations. Thus, they are not for the most part permitted to exchange on the NYSE or the NASDAQ. All things considered, they exchange on the OTCBB ("over the counter notice board") or Pink Sheets, the two of which have considerably less rigid monetary announcing prerequisites than the significant trades do.

A considerable lot of these organizations have never made a benefit. They might be fakes or shell organizations that are planned exclusively to improve the board and different insiders. They may likewise incorporate previous "blue-chips" that have run into some bad luck like Eastman Kodak or Lehman Brothers. What's more, penny stocks are characteristically more unstable than more extravagant stocks. Consider it along these lines: if a $100 stock moves $1, that is a 1% move. In the event that a $5 stock moves $1, that is a 20% move. Numerous new brokers belittle the sort of enthusiastic and monetary harm that this sort of instability can cause. Watcher caution is exhorted.

3. Try not to short stocks

In the event that you are a high-level merchant, do not hesitate to disregard this standard. In the event that you are not, I would truly urge you not to disregard this standard.

To short a stock, you should initially get portions of the stock from your specialist. You at that point sell those offers on the open market. On the off chance that the stock falls in value, you will actually want to repurchase those offers at a lower cost for a benefit.

Assuming, be that as it may, the stock goes up a great deal, you might be compelled to repurchase the offers at a lot greater cost, and wind up losing more cash than you ever had in your exchanging record in any case.

In November 2015, Joe Campbell broke 2 of the 5 precepts. He previously chose to exchange a penny stock called KaloBios Pharmaceuticals. To exacerbate the situation, he chose to short it.

At the point when he hit the sack that night, his exchanging account was worth generally $37,000. At the point when he woke up the following morning, the stock had soared. Thus, not just had he lost the entirety of the $37,000, however he currently owed his intermediary an extra $106,000.

What's more, there was no chance to get out. On the off chance that you owe your dealer cash, they can pull you into court and pursue your home and reserve funds.

Now and then even the most affluent investors can be cleared out by shorting a stock. During the incomparable Northern Pacific Corner of 1901, portions of that railroad stock went from $170 to $1,000 in a solitary day. That move bankrupted the absolute most well-off Americans of the day, who had shorted the stock and were then compelled to cover at greater costs.

In the event that you do wind up shorting a stock, recollect that your representative will charge you an expense (normally communicated as a yearly financing cost) to acquire the stock. Also, in the event that you are short a stock, you are liable for delivering any profits on that stock (your specialist will naturally remove the cash from your record quarterly).

For these reasons, shorting stocks is obviously a high level and hazardous exchanging procedure. Try not to attempt it until you have been exchanging for in any event 5 years, and you have the monetary soundness to withstand a stunning upwards move in a stock.

Furthermore, never short a penny stock. It is simply not justified, despite the potential benefits.

4. Try not to exchange on edge

To short a stock, you should open up an edge account with your merchant, as Joe Campbell did. You will likewise require an edge account to exchange stocks utilizing edge.

At the point when you purchase a stock on edge, it implies that you are acquiring cash from your intermediary, to buy a bigger number of portions of stock than you would typically have the option to purchase with simply the money sitting in your investment fund. Suppose that I have $10,000 in my edge account. Most agents in the U.S. will permit me to go on edge to buy $20,000 worth of stock in that account. This means they are loaning me an extra $10,000 (for the most part at some over the top yearly loan cost like 11%, which is the thing that E*TRADE presently charges) to purchase more portions of stock. In the event that I purchase $10,000 worth of stock and the stock goes up 10%, I've quite recently made $1,000. However, on the off chance that I can build the measure of stock that I'm purchasing to $20,000 utilizing an edge advance, I will have made $2,000 on a similar 10% move. That will imply that my exchanging account has quite recently gone up by 20% ($2,000/$10,000). Obviously, if the stock goes down 10% and I'm on full edge, I will have lost 20% of my record esteem. Exchanging on edge is accordingly a type of influence: it enhances the exhibition of your portfolio both on the potential gain and the drawback.

At the point when you purchase a stock utilizing edge, the stock and money in your exchanging account are held as security for the edge advance. On the off chance that the stock falls enough, you might be needed to add more money to your record quickly (this is called "getting an edge call"), or danger having the specialist drive you to promptly offer your stock to raise money. Frequently this will prompt your selling the stock at the absolute worst time. At the point when you open up another investment fund and you are given the decision of a "money account" or an "edge account," it's OK to pick "edge account". An edge account has certain favorable circumstances, for example, having the option to utilize the returns from offering a stock to quickly purchase another stock without trusting that the exchange will settle. In the event that you never surpass your money purchasing influence in an edge account, you won't ever be charged expenses or premium. In that manner, it is very conceivable to have an edge account, however never to go on edge. Assuming, in any case, you don't confide in yourself, open up a "money account". That way, you won't ever be permitted to exchange on edge.

5. Try not to exchange others' thoughts

The primary explanation never to exchange another person's thoughts is that they presumably don't have the foggiest idea of what they are doing. On the off chance that you get a hot stock tip from your neighbor or at the rec center, it's ideal to overlook it. They likely have no clue about the thing they are discussing.

Second, regardless of whether you get a great and genuine exchanging or investing thought from another person, you will presumably not have the conviction to clutch it when difficulties arise. That conviction can just come from building up an exchange thought yourself. At the point when you have planned an exchange, or investigated an investment for yourself, you will have the conviction to hang on. You will likewise know where your stop misfortune is, on the off chance that the stock goes south. Have you seen how hot stock tips never accompanied a suggested stop misfortune level?

Additionally, never place an exchange dependent on something that you have recently perused in Barron's, Forbes, The Wall Street Journal, or have quite recently seen on CNBC. Never purchase a stock dependent on an expert redesign, or sell a stock dependent on an investigator downsize. I have seen investigators at last minimization a stock just whenever it has fallen half.

Investigators are slacking markers. They will in general overhaul stocks that have just gone up, and downsize stocks that have just dropped down. There is likewise a solid choice predisposition among experts. The best experts get employed by mutual funds, and you never get with them again. The most exceedingly terrible investigators stay at the banks or business houses, and keep on administering their unremarkable guidance. Gigantic measures of cash have been lost by following their recommendation. Would it be a good idea for you to try and follow Warren Buffett's recommendation, as I proposed in a past part? Indeed, and no. His recommendation is unquestionably far superior to a hot stock tip from your neighbor. Then again, in the event that you tuned in to him strictly, you passed up the entirety of the incredible tech stocks of the most recent 20 years. He held up until Apple and Amazon were up a huge number of rate focuses before at long last buying them. Anybody can figure out how to think for themselves in the securities exchange, and concoct their own exchanging and investing thoughts. That is the objective behind the entirety of my books and exchanging courses. Instead of giving you a fish, I would much rather show you how to look for yourself. That is the way to genuine independence from the rat race.

Mistakes that even Good Investors had Made

It's not easy to save your money and invest it wisely, especially with economic trends changing all the time. However, there are many pitfalls even for expert investors to avoid that can keep both your wealth and peace of mind intact.

Carelessness

Carelessness is perhaps the most common mistake, and it's usually made when you're fired up by a hot stock tip. This leads to buying and holding onto stocks that are overvalued, or even worse, heavily invested in one single company's shares. You've got to remain rational when investing, and not just focus on how much the company can make you profit. Be realistic about what your expectations will be before getting involved in any investment opportunity.

Overconfidence

Overconfidence is a big danger for those who invest in the stock market independently without any advice or support from experts. The danger stems from the belief that one is smart enough to pick winning stocks without any assistance. Of course, that is impossible—since nobody really knows the future, it is important to pay attention to potential investment opportunities and keep an eye on your investments.

Not Paying Attention to the Company's Condition

A company's assets may be increasing in value and their business may be developing nicely; however, there are some red flags in their current operations that you need to pay attention to. A good example of this is watching the trend of a company's ratio of profit margin versus its asset turnover ratio.

If the profit margin remains stable while the asset turnover ratio keeps decreasing or just stays flat then it's an indication that management isn't putting money into research & development for expansion or merger opportunities—a big warning sign.

Lack of Diversification

Many people only invest in the stock market because they want to get rich quick. This is an unwise idea, because greed often leads to investing in only one or two companies that appear to be growing quickly but have nothing behind them.

Sure, one or two companies may appear golden right now; however, you need to remain diversified so that if the business fails you won't be left with nothing.

Stock Trading without a Plan

Many people don't have a plan when it comes to investing and just buy stocks on whim and base their decisions off of no information at all. This is a very risky way to invest, as you may end up losing all of your money. When investing, you need to have a solid plan that takes into account the trends of the market and how you will benefit from investing in stocks.

Trying to Time the Market

There is never any surefire way to predict when the stock market will rise or fall, so many investors take this lack of knowledge as an opportunity to make quick money by timing the market.

This is dangerous and should be avoided at all costs—if you want to make money in the stock market then do so by investing for the long run and not hoping for short-term gains.

Swing Trading

Some investors get involved in "swing trading"—they buy when the market is low and sell when it rises. This can be a profitable strategy, but only if you are experienced and have a deep understanding of the market. However, it is very risky because if you are wrong even once then you can lose all of your money. Even professional stock traders advise against swing trading, so don't even try it unless you've got lots of practice doing it right.

Keep All Your Eggs in One Basket

This is a very common expression that is often used to describe investing in the stock market. The most common way to put this into practice is by not investing too heavily in any one company, or even worse, investing your life savings into a single company. This can be very risky and it's easy to lose everything if you're not careful.

Watching the Volume

Investors often watch the volume of shares being traded for a certain stock because they want to know how many people are buying and selling stock at any given time. This is a very risky strategy that is difficult to make money off of because the volume of shares related to a company is usually dependent on their growth—if they're not growing then there won't be as many people investing in their stock.

Warren Miller

CHAPTER 15

Chapter 15. Insider's Secret of the Stock Market

Allow me to begin by helping you to remember quite possibly the main realities about the stock market: *Response to the news is in every case more significant than the actual news.*

Thus, likewise: *Response to an income report is in every case more significant than the profit report itself.*

It's quite often a bearish sign when a stock auctions after a decent income report. On the off chance that a stock that has had a major run-up falls on a decent profit report, it very well might be an indication that the upturn is finished.

The inverse is likewise obvious. At the point when a stock actually revitalizes after an "awful" profit report, it is a bullish sign. It's additionally a bullish sign if the stock market rallies after a negative financial report.

Numerous individuals get difficult and attempt to guide the stock market. Savvy dealers tune in to the market all things being equal.

Because you need to bring in cash today doesn't imply that the chance will be naturally accessible. You should figure out how to be content with what the market is at present ready to offer you. Try not to drive an exchange. Be patient, and sit tight for the fat pitch. On the off chance that you can learn persistence and order, the market will at last reward you beyond anything you could ever imagine. Zero in on a couple of stocks, and become more acquainted with how they exchange. Try not to extend yourself excessively far by attempting to follow such a large number of stocks. On the off chance that you have committed an error, cut your misfortunes rapidly and proceed onward. Never let an exchange transform into a drawn-out investment. Try not to average exchanging misfortunes. Try not to squander valuable resources. Never add to a losing position, however don't hesitate to add to a position once it begins to bring in cash.

The stock market is a limiting machine. That implies that it takes all accessible data about an organization and the economy and changes a stock's cost in like manner. In some cases it makes a preferable showing of this over different occasions. The stock market tends to over-markdown recognized dangers, and under-rebate unidentified dangers.

At whatever point you continue to find out about a danger in the monetary news, it is in all likelihood previously valued into a stock, or the stock market all in all. The dangers you are not hearing anything about, or that appear to be ludicrously far-fetched, that can cause the most harm. In the event that everybody is looking at something, it's quite often as of now estimated into the market. That implies that the stock has just moved to where it should be, founded on the entirety of the data that is as of now accessible. To bring in cash in exchanging or investing, you need to skate to where the puck will be, not to where it has just been.

A market that consistently neglects to move higher will typically go down. The stock market (just as individual stocks) will consistently look out our weaknesses, and move so as to make the most extreme agony the greatest number of merchants.

Temporarily, mass brain science manages the markets, not essentials or the economy. Improving organization essentials and great monetary news will frequently appear in stock costs before they appear in the features, which is the reason it is so imperative to follow through on regard for cost activity.

However long the market is going up, and your stock is going up, don't be in a rush to take benefits. To dominate at this match, you should have a few huge victors. Try not to interfere with them too early.

There is an irregularity to the stock market that we ought not disregard. Albeit the two most well-known stock market declines both happened in October (1929 and 1987), September has generally been the most fragile month for the stock market. Normal recorded returns for June and August are additionally negative. This has prompted the renowned articulation "Sell in May and disappear". Stock market gets back from November through April have verifiably been a lot higher than stock market gets back from May through October. This doesn't really imply that you should offer the entirety of your stocks and go to money each May. However, it implies that you ought to be more careful when exchanging throughout the mid-year months. Numerous merchants and investors are at the seashore, so liquidity is lower and instability is higher. On the off chance that you are searching for a decent long-haul investment, purchase an organization that has the most elevated deals in its industry. So, for home improvement, you need to possess Home Depot; for inexpensive food, McDonald's; for toothpaste, Colgate Palmolive; for installments, Visa; for PDAs, Apple; and for online media, Facebook.

When a business sells more than some other organization in its industry, it turns out to be hard to rival. There's not a viable replacement for being #1 in your industry.

At the point when the entirety of the specialists concurs, at that point something other than what's expected will occur in the market. The current customary way of thinking is in every case previously evaluated into the market.

Here is a portion of my record-breaking most loved statements about exchanging and the stock market:

- George Soros: *"It's not whether you're correct or wrong that is significant, but rather how much cash you make when you're correct and the amount you lose when you're off-base."*
- John Maynard Keynes: *"Markets can stay nonsensical longer than you can stay dissolvable."*
- Dennis Gartman: *"The markets will get back to soundness the second that you have been delivered bankrupt."*
- William Eckhardt: *"Either an exchange is sufficient to take, in which case it ought to be actualized at full size, or it's not worth wasting time with by any means."*
- Ed Seykota: *"Basics that you read about are ordinarily pointless as the market has just limited the cost, and I call them 'clever mentals'. I am basically a pattern merchant with bits of hunches dependent on around twenty years of involvement. Arranged by significance to me are: (1) the drawn-out pattern, (2) the current diagram example, and (3) picking a decent spot to purchase or sell. Those are the three essential segments of my exchanging. Path down in far off fourth spot are my crucial thoughts and, very likely, on equilibrium, they have cost me cash."*
- Jim Rogers: *"I simply stand by until there is cash lying in the corner, and I should simply go over yonder and get it. I don't do anything meanwhile. Indeed, even individuals who lose cash in the market say, 'I just lost my cash, presently I need to plan something to make it back.' No, you don't. You ought to stay there until you discover something."*

- Bruce Kovner: *"At whatever point I enter a position, I have a foreordained stop. That is the lone way I can rest. I realize where I'm getting out before I get in. The position size on an exchange is dictated by the stop, and the stop is resolved on a specialized premise."*

- Paul Tudor Jones: *"Don't be a saint. Try not to have a sense of self. Continuously question yourself and your capacity. Never feel that you are excellent. The subsequent you do, you are dead. My greatest hits have consistently come after I have had an incredible period and I began to believe that I knew something."*

- Ed Seykota*: "The way to long haul endure and thrive has a great deal to do with the cash the executives' strategies consolidated into the specialized framework. There are old brokers and there are striking dealers, however there are not many old, intense merchants."*

- *Bulls bring in cash, bears bring in cash, however pigs get butchered*. I have heard this old Wall Street maxim very often: it is a warns against greed and impatience of certain investors, represented by the pigs, whose goal is to make the most amount of money in the shortest amount of time. As a result, they tend to lose money, so they get slaughtered.

Warren Miller

CHAPTER 16

Some of the Top Traders in the Stock Market

Benjamin Graham

Benjamin Graham was born in 1894 in London, United Kingdom. When he was still a child, his family moved to America, where they lost their savings during the 1907 Bank Panic. Graham graduated from Columbia University and began working on Wall Street with Newburger, Henderson and Loeb. At the age of 25, he was already earning around $ 500,000 a year.

In the 1929 stock market crash, Graham lost nearly all of his investments, which taught him some valuable lessons about the world of investing.

His observations after the crash inspired him to write a book with David Dodd, called *"Security Analysis"* first published in 1934, which outlined the fundamental basis of investing in value, which involves buying undervalued stocks. with the potential for growth over time.

According to Graham and Dodd, the investment of value derives from the intrinsic value of an ordinary share independent of its market price. Using factors of a company such as its assets, earnings, and dividend payments, the intrinsic value of a stock can be found and compared with its market value. If the intrinsic value is higher than the current price, the investor should buy and hold until a return to the average occurs. A return to the average is the theory according to which over time the market price and the intrinsic price will converge towards each other until the share price reflects its true value.

In 1949, Graham wrote the famous book *"The Intelligent Investor: The Definitive Book on Value Investing"*, considered the bible of value investing and presents a character known as Mr. Market as a metaphor for the mechanics of market prices.

Graham points out that instead of relying on the daily market sentiments which are driven by the investor's emotions of greed and fear, the investor should perform their own analysis of the value of a stock based on the company's reports on its operations and financial position.

This analysis should reinforce the investor's judgment when he made an offer. According to Graham, the smart investor is the one who sells to the optimists and buys from the pessimists. The investor should look for opportunities to buy low and sell high.

Warren Buffet

With regards to offering monetary guidance, barely any individuals can enthrall a group of people very like Warren Buffet can. His uncommon achievement in the realm of investments—also his $85 billion fortune—implies even those not a tiny smidgen inspired by money sit up and listen when Buffett shares his top tips for accumulating riches.

However Buffett is something beyond the amount of his bank balance (a ten-figure number to be careful). His life is covered in an energy for business and investments and, notwithstanding his tremendous riches, he is broadly known for his liberality and thriftiness—he actually lives in the very home in Omaha in Nebraska that he purchased for $31,000 in 1958 and all the more as of late he has vowed to part with 99% of his abundance to noble cause.

His story is a captivating one without a doubt. Who is Warren Buffet? What is a portion of his rules that you can apply in your life and business? What would you be able to gain from Buffett's own encounters about dealing with your life, cash and vocation?

Buffett has just stood up to and beaten life's difficulties and made a way that could fill in as a triumphant guide for you. You should simply follow that way on your approach to progress. You'll have to change and modify it a little to meet your own circumstances and conditions, however the outline is to a great extent set up. Throughout everyday life and business, you can benefit as much as possible from the intelligence learned by effective and affluent individuals who have made an imprint for themselves around the world and use it as a manual for accomplishing your own objectives.

For quite a long time, Buffett has been a good example to thousands, if not millions, of growing business visionaries and individuals quick to have an effect in their lives. His prosperity has affected the activities of finance managers all around the planet and has filled in as an uncommon norm to take a stab at both expertly and by and by, gratitude to his liberality and eagerness to help other people. His impact spreads all over and even those among the most extravagant on the planet have received Buffett's life draws near. Because of Buffett's consolation, for instance, in excess of 160 very rich people have consented to give and part with at any rate half of their abundance for humanitarian causes.

Paul Tudor Jones

Paul Tudor Jones is an American Investor, a mutual funds administrator and he is otherwise called a humanitarian. Jones was brought into the world on September 28th, 1954. His adoration for Hedge store on the board drove him to open his firm back in 1980, an organization by the name Tudor Investment Corporation. The organization's central command is as yet situated in Greenwich, associate cut, and it had some expertise in the administration of resources. Later on, he made Tudor gathering which is a speculative stock investments Holding Company. The Tudor fence organization worked in the administration of fixed pay, monetary standards, values and furthermore products.

Throughout the most recent years, his organizations have been doing extraordinary procuring him incredible fortunes since in February 2017, he was assessed to have a net of 4.7 billion by Forbes magazine and this caused him to be number 120 the of the richest individuals on the planet on the class of 400 individuals positioned on the magazine.

Tim Cook

Timothy Donald Cook is the American leader, Industrial Engineer, and Developer. He is at present the Chief boss at the workplaces of Apple Inc. This is the new position he gained at the Apple Inc. since he recently functioned as the Chief Operating Officer under the originator Steve Jobs. Joined Apple in the year 1998 as the senior VP of overall tasks and afterward he later filled in as the chief VP of the world in the division of deals and administrations. On March 24th, 2011, he was elevated to turn into the Chief leader. He is associated with his dynamic advocating of different mankind and natural development which incorporate the transformation of political of global and nearby observation, online protection, enterprise tax assessment both broadly and universally. Condition's conservation and furthermore the American assembling act.

In the year 2014, Cook became public and recognized himself as gay and was recorded among the 500 CEO at Fortune magazine. Different organizations that Cook worked at incorporate; he was an individual from the leading group of sheets of heads of Nike-Inc., the public football establishment, the trustee of Duke University.

Around 2012, the Apple Inc. organization chose to give Cook a pay of offers worth huge number of dollars vesting in 2016 to 2021. During a public discourse, Cook said that his income from the allowed stocks would be offered to good cause establishments. This incorporates all that he possesses.

George Soros

George Soros is one of the thirty richest men on Earth. He is estimated to have a net worth of $ 25 billion.

Born in Budapest in 1930 to a family of Jewish origin, Soros emigrated to England after surviving the Nazi occupation of Hungary. He graduated from the London School of Economics and then completed a Master in Philosophy.

In 1969, after making his way through various commercial banks, Soros together with Jim Rogers founded the first Double Eagle hedge fund (after renamed Quantum Fund), with a financial endowment of 4 million dollars of capital from investors and 250,000 dollars by way of personal assets.

In 2011, the same fund allowed him to reach $ 25 billion.

Soros is known as the man who got rich by engaging in a series of financial speculations, such as the 1992 short-selling of pounds and lira, which disrupted their respective national governments and banks and earned them billions of dollars.

The concept of reflexivity developed by finance has changed the foundations of the economy. "*When markets rise or fall rapidly, they are characterized by imbalances and conventional economic theory does not have to be applied*" he argues.

In *"The New Paradigm for Financial Markets"* published in May 2008, Soros describes a "super-bubble" that has developed over the previous 25 years and was poised to explode. It was a good prediction: after all, the tycoon never got one wrong.

Carl Icahn

Carl Icahn was brought into the world on Feb 16, 1936, and he is a notable money manager in America. Aside from possessing a few organizations, he was likewise and still most popular for being a sensible investor and givers as well. He established the

Icahn Enterprises, and he is the regulator of all the organization's offer since he is the biggest investor. The organization is huge, and it is situated in the New York City. Of late the organization is known as the combination Holding organization, however at first, it was alluded to as American Real bequest Partners. Cahn has additionally led the Federal-Mogul organization, which works in creating, fabricating and furthermore providing the powertrain parts and vehicle security items.

Carl has additionally won hearts of numerous because of his business strategies whereby he was named as the corporate bandit because of his capacity to benefit from the threatening takeover and the resource depriving of the American aircraft. Forbes magazine took a gander at his abundance, and he is assessed to have a sum of 16.6 billion dollars by 2017. He was additionally positioned as number 26 of the most well-off individuals in work on the 400 rich individuals classes. In the support business world, Carl has all the earmarks of being on top five of most well-off men taking the last position.

John C. Bogle

John C. Bogle was born on May 8, 1929, in Montclair, New Jersey to William Yates Bogle Jr. and Josephine Lorraine Hipkins. In 1947 he graduated with honors and was admitted to Princeton University, where he studied economics. During his university years, Bogle studied the mutual fund sector and the link between the cost of a financial product and its profitability: in a sector that was becoming increasingly competitive, being able to do better than the market would always have been more difficult, therefore, it was better to exactly replicate the returns by reducing the difference due to management costs.

In 1951 Walter L. Morgan hired him. In 1970 he replaced Morgan as Wellington's president. He was later fired for an "extremely reckless" merger that he approved.

On May 1, 1975, Bogle founded the Vanguard Company, which is one of the most respected and successful companies in the investment world today.

In 1999 he wrote " *The Little Book of Common Sense on Mutual Funds: New Imperatives for the Intelligent Investor*" which became a classic in the financial community and a best-seller. In the same year, Fortune magazine named Bogle "one of the four investment giants of the twentieth century."

In 2001, he founded the First Index Investment Trust, a precursor to the Vanguard 500 Index Fund, as the first mutual fund available to the general public. The fund replicated the performance of the S&P 500 index and was the first index fund to be sold among retail investors and not just institutional ones. Bogle's innovative idea was to create the first index mutual fund, actually born in 1975. Bogle believed that, instead of beating the index and charging high costs, the index fund would mimic the performance of the index. 'index over the long term, thus achieving higher returns with lower costs than those of actively managed funds.

His ideas were so innovative that they led to the founding of the "Bogleheads" movement, a group of individual investors who still today follow the basic principles of his philosophy: start saving when young, diversify, seek simplicity and stay true to their plan. financial regardless of market conditions.

Warren Miller

Conclusion

Congratulations for making it to the end. Financial freedom is a long play game in that once you achieve it; you can sit back and enjoy the fruits of your labor. However, before you can reach financial freedom you must first learn to live below your means. This means that for all expenses (not just housing) you spend no more than 60% of your take-home pay. The reason for this is that if an emergency arises, or someone in the family gets sick, or there are other unexpected expenses, then there will be money set aside to take care of these challenges. Next, it is important to determine which expenses are fixed (such as mortgage and utility bills) and which are flexible (such as food and clothing). It is important to practice spending as if everything is flexible except the fixed expenses. It is easy to overspend and ignore the fixed expense portion of your budget, but this can cause a serious cash flow issue as you try to figure out where that money came from. Once you have mastered living below your means and determining fixed expenses, it is time to focus on creating income sources that are not salary-dependent. Many people have these types of accounts but still rely primarily on their salary from their day job for household income. Investing your money for retirement or starting a small business creates an income source that is not salary-dependent. This is important because once you reach retirement age, if you cannot get another job, you will be able to live off of the investments you have made for your retirement. Once these two areas are mastered, it is time to create additional sources of income. These may include writing eBooks, selling digital products like online courses, or becoming a consultant for other business owners and professionals. Financial freedom requires that you have multiple streams of income coming in, so that if one area slows down for any reason there are other options that continue to give you an income stream. Don't be fooled… Financial freedom is possible.

If you are still skeptical about the possibility of achieving this goal, here are some quick facts:

- 75% of U.S. citizens are living paycheck to paycheck
- 56% have less than $1,000 in savings, 5% have no savings at all
- 34% of U.S. citizens haven't had a raise in the past five years
- 40 million workers (out of the 120 million) don't have any type of retirement plan set up at their jobs
- 1 out of 5 workers 55 or older say they have no retirement savings or pension

As you can see, there is a definite need to get your financial future moving in the right direction, and it's never too late to turn things around for yourself and your family.

But is financial freedom really possible? Absolutely! There are several key steps to make it happen:

1. Make a list of all your expenses and commitments. This will help you figure out where you're spending your money, how much you have left over, and where you can cut back. Once the numbers are in front of you, see if there is anything that can be cut back or eliminated altogether. Only after taking a hard look at your situation will you be able to figure out any ways that may help save some money or get yourself in a better financial position.

2. Use the "Pay Yourself First" Principle to Budget Your Money. Pay yourself first by putting money away before you pay your bills or take care of your other financial commitments. The idea is to put a portion of the money you make into an "emergency fund" and/or retirement account.

This way, if something comes up unexpectedly, you don't have to worry about paying for it on credit or dipping into your savings. You have already taken care of it ahead of time.

3. Avoid debt as soon as possible. If there are any debts that you carry around from month-to-month, start attacking those first in order to get them out of the way faster (and to avoid interest charges). The longer you let debt go, the more expensive it gets.

4. Start putting money into your retirement account. One of the best ways to begin is to start up a Roth IRA (Roth Individual Retirement Account). With a Roth IRA, you can withdraw money without having to pay any penalties or interest on it if you need it for certain expenses (such as college tuition). You'll also have the freedom to use that money whenever and however you wish in retirement (since by then it will be yours!).

5. Remember that successful saving depends on your buying power, not the number of years you work. A person who begins saving at age 25 (with a 5% savings rate) will have 50% more purchasing power than someone who waits until age 35 to save.

6. Don't be afraid to take risks. Let's face it—no matter how much money you might make, there are times when you just don't have any left over each month after all your bills and other financial commitments are taken care of. If this is just like your situation, you need to start thinking outside the box, and that means taking some calculated risks. Start investing in income-producing real estate (even if it's just a modest investment) or start your own business. The rewards can be great, but only if you take the risk!

7. Don't give up! If you don't see results in the beginning, don't give up! Give yourself some time to make things happen and keep working towards your goal.

In order to achieve financial freedom, you have to stop blaming others for your problems and start taking responsibility for your own life. Commit yourself to your ultimate goal of achieving financial freedom, and you'll be one step closer to achieving your dreams!

Risks of Not Investing

You Don't Have a Plan

If you don't have an investment plan in place, you are really just guessing about where you think your money will be in the future. Why not take a bit of time to figure out what's important to you now and determine how long you would like your money to last?

You're Lacking Long-Term Goals

If there are no big goals in your life, then there is also no need for long-term planning and investing. Luckily, you have time, but setting out some goals today is a great way to keep your motivation up and give yourself a clear vision of what your future looks like.

The Downside of Investing

Investing in the stock market can be terrifying, there is no doubt about that. If you start taking a look at the past performance of the stock market and see some really bad years, it can certainly make you wary of making investments today. Don't let this get to you—stocks have more good years than they do bad; historically speaking (according to Yale University). From 1871-2014, the average annualized return on stocks was 7%.

Wall Street

If you are hesitant about investing in the stock market because you do not understand Wall Street, then this is another reason why you need to take some time to learn more about how it works.

You're Too Afraid to Invest

This may sound silly, but some people are too afraid to invest because they think it will cost too much or take too much work. There is an old saying that goes something like *"you miss 100% of the shots you never take"*. If you're looking for more information, we recommend checking out this post from Carl Richards that outlines all the reasons you're too afraid to invest.

You Don't Have a Plan B

Having a plan is important, but even more important ois knowing what will happen if your plan doesn't work out. Having an investment plan in place is great, but if something happens and your investments drop dramatically, it's good to have some sort of backup plan so that you can adjust accordingly. This could mean laying out another investment plan with new goals or cutting back on your spending until your portfolio recovers.

You Think It's Too Complicated

If you are worried about the intricacies of the market, don't be. Investing is actually quite simple if you just start with a few basic steps. As you gain more confidence and momentum, you can add additional investments to your portfolio, but it is important to start small and work your way up to larger portfolios over time.

You Don't Have the Time

This is another misconception that some people have about investing: that it takes too much time or that they don't have enough time for all their other responsibilities and commitments in life. If you are working more than 40 hours a week, then you've got some extra time to devote to investing. It's important to make the time, especially if you are trying to build wealth and save for your future.

You Lack Control

If you are averse to investing because you feel like your money is just going into some black hole and there is nothing that can be done about it, then this is another misconception that needs to be cleared up. Investing in the stock market will give you more control than any other investment vehicle out there—if something goes wrong with one of your stocks or funds, then it will correct over time and you can sell it at a profit (or loss).

You're Afraid to Make an Investment Mistake

This is another big fear that keeps people from investing: that they will make a mistake and lose all their money. This is not very likely if you are using an investment professional or do some sort of due diligence on your own before you invest.

Appendix

Recommended Readings and Podcasts

Investing is a new, daunting field for many people. In many ways, it is much harder to learn about investing than about someone's passion for science or art. It requires a lot of time and dedication that not everyone can afford to dedicate to just one thing. But if you're interested in learning more about investing, the following reads and podcasts should give you a good start! They range from short reads all the way to hour-long podcasts with interviews of investment professionals all over the world.

The following is a list of recommended books. While they are absolute must-reads in order to learn about investing, recommended for those looking to take their knowledge of investing to the next level.

Investing Books

- *John C. Bogle on Investing: The First 50 Years*—Reflections of the Dean of Vanguard and Index Investing (Second Edition). This book gives you a history lesson on how Mr. Bogle got where he is today, as well as various insights into his thoughts on investing. It's written in a more casual format, and is both insightful and interesting.

- *The Little Book of Common Sense Investing* by John C. Bogle. This little book is the "bible" for value-driven investing. While it's a bit dry in places, it also contains Mr. Bogle's thoughts on why indexing is so important, how to tell good investments from bad ones, and many other things that are useful for beginners down the road. I'd suggest reading it when you've already got a good grasp on Bogle head investing and want to know a bit more about the man who pioneered value-driven investing.

- *The Future for Investors: Why the Tried and True Triumphs over the Bold and New* by Jeremy Siegel. Published in 2006, this book is no longer up to date on market trends. However, as one of the books that helped popularize "value" investing, it's still relevant today even if it has some outdated examples.

- *The Latte Factor* by David Bach and John David Mann: This book show some finance key concepts and secrets to financial freedom with an engaging story. It is a nice book to start to familiarize with compounding interest and the *"Pay Yourself First"* Principle.

- *The Intelligent Investor* by Benjamin Graham: This is a classic, a book that has earned its place in the literary canon for financial titles for many good reasons.

- *Why Didn't They Teach Me This in School?* By Cary Siegel: This is a fun and very easy book to read with many principles, good advice, and lessons about money and personal finance written by a retired business executive.

Podcasts

- *Invest Like the Best*—A lot of people talk a big game about investing, but few have actually done it. The guys at *"Invest Like the Best"* have invested with some of the best in the world, allowing you to get their insights from their experiences. Recommended for those who want to learn more about what it's like to be an investor in 2018.

- *The Investors Podcast*—More of a novice podcast, this one focuses on teaching beginner investors how to take their first investment steps. It doesn't get into too much nitty-gritty or advanced topics (which is good for beginners), but it covers a lot of useful information, nonetheless.

- *The Invested Investor*—A podcast more geared towards financial advisors, *The Invested Investor* focuses on interviews with professionals in the field and their thoughts on investment strategy.

- *Mad Money with Jim Cramer* - This popular podcast guides auditors through the mistakes and good opportunities of Wall Street, exploring with the goal of helping them make money.

One Last Tip for You

Many people think that financial freedom is just a pipe dream, something that it's impossible to achieve. But the truth is, achieving financial freedom requires only one thing. Commitment!

It takes commitment and perseverance to get any goal you want in life, whether it's getting a good job or losing weight.

Financial freedom takes the same commitment as anything else: all you need to do is figure out what works best for you and keep at it!

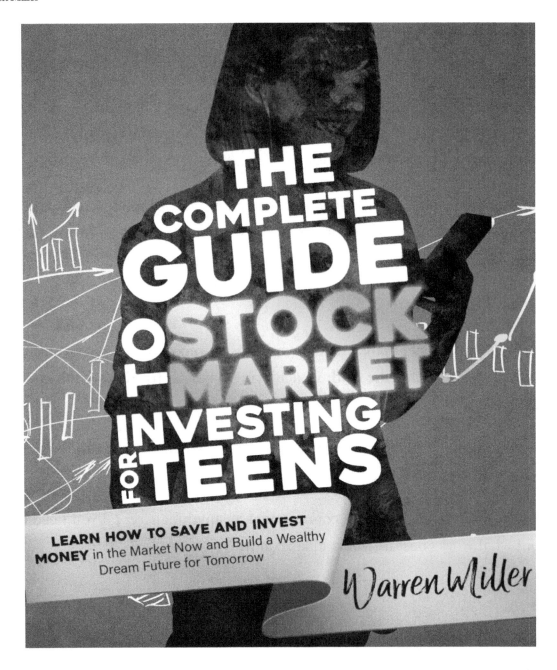

From the same Author

Available on AMAZON

Made in United States
North Haven, CT
05 December 2021